If you can enjoy the sun and flowers and music where there is nothing except darkness and silence you have proved the Mystic Sense _____ Helen Keller

S0-AXJ-489

In 1918 Miss Keller went to California to play a role in a silent film and is shown here with Miss Polly Thomson (*left*) Anne Sullivan (*right*) and comedian Charlie Chaplin.

Mr. John Hitz, Miss Keller's "Spiritual Godfather."

"One thing I know
. . .Whereas I was blind
Now I see"

# MY RELIGION

*Helen Keller*

SWEDENBORG FOUNDATION, INC.

17th Printing 1986

Standard Book Number 0—87785—103—4
Library of Congress Catalog Card Number 74—11645

*Cover art by B. Forbes*
*Photographs courtesy of the American Foundation for the Blind*

Manufactured in the United States of America

SWEDENBORG FOUNDATION, INC.
139 East 23rd Street
New York, New York 10010 USA

# HELEN KELLER

*was born in 1880. Before she was two years old, she lost her eyesight and hearing through an illness. "For nearly six years," she says, "I had no concepts whatever of nature or mind or death or God. I literally thought with my body. Without a single exception my memories of that time are tactual . . . there is not one spark of emotion or rational thought in these distinct, yet corporal memories. I was like an unconscious clod of earth. Then, suddenly, I knew not how or where or when, my brain felt the impact of another mind, and I awoke to language, to knowledge of love, to the usual concepts of nature, of good and evil."*

*Slowly, painfully, she learned the names of the things she could touch; she learned to talk and to listen with her hands. She learned to read—to write and typewrite; she was admitted to Radcliffe College, and studied there. No woman of any age has been more justly celebrated.*

*Cut off from the world of light and sound, her spiritual perceptions are correspondingly acute. She understands Swedenborg's visions of good and evil spirits, for her life is spent on a spiritual plane. The gift of Helen Keller's book is the firm knowledge of the spiritual* world, where she lives immune from the distractions of the physical world—and the courage and faith that come as a result of this knowledge.

# FOREWORD

HELEN KELLER was loved the world over. Her accomplishments in the face of unique difficulties have stirred our sense of the heroic; her patient struggle and convincing triumph touched our hearts. No one can appreciate the secret of her growth without some knowledge of her spiritual background. To her, religion was a way of living day by day. In her view, spiritual life was as real and as practical as natural life. Her Christianity was built on the gospel of love.

Miss Keller was often questioned in public about her religion. She answered briefly, but always longed to say more. And so, when asked to write a book about her religion, she welcomed the opportunity to tell her many friends just what her religious ideals were and where she found them. It was a labor of love, and she poured her soul into it, not to argue a point, but to share with others what was of inestimable value to her.

Here is a mind kept singularly pure from childhood; here is a religious experience unhampered by the blindness of any sectarianism; here is a spiritual insight, a gift of perception, undulled by absorption in the things of sense life. Here is one in whom the Lord has worked a miracle, and she declares to us "One thing I know, that whereas I was blind, now I see."

Paul Sperry

Washington, D.C.

## SWEDENBORG

*"Heaven unbarred to him her lofty gates."*

   O light-bringer of my blindness,
O spirit never far removed!
Ever when the hour of travail deepens,
Thou art near;
Set in my soul like jewels bright
Thy words of holy meaning,
Till Death with gentle hand shall lead me
   to the Presence I have loved—
My torch in darkness here,
My joy eternal there.

HELEN KELLER

# MY
# RELIGION

# I

HANS ANDERSON describes in one of his beautiful tales a garden where giant trees grew out of pots that were too small for them. Their roots were cruelly cramped; yet they lifted themselves up bravely into the sunlight, flung abroad their glorious branches, showered their wealth of blossoms and refreshed weary mortals with their golden fruit. Into their hospitable arms came all singing birds, and ever in their hearts was a song of renewal and joy. At last they burst the hard, cold shackles that confined them and spread out their mighty roots in the sweetness of liberty.

To my mind that strange garden symbolizes the Eighteenth Century out of which grew the Titan genius of Emanuel Swedenborg. Some call that century the Age of Reason, and characterize it as the coldest, most depressing time recorded in human history. It is true, progress was wonderful everywhere. There were great philosophers, and statesmen, and fearless investigators in science. Governments were better organized, the feudal system was held in check, and the public highways rendered more safe than they had ever been. The fiery passions of mediævalism were curbed by a severe decorum and the iron sceptre of reason.

But at that period, as in the Dark Ages before it, there was a sinister, oppressive atmosphere of sadness and sullen resignation. Able writers like Taine in his history of literature have noted how a bitter theology treated man as a despised child of sin and gave the world over to the wrath of God. Even the gentle angel, Charity, whom the saints of old had welcomed, was driven from man's side; faith alone was exalted, and not faith either, but a self-centred assumption that belief alone was necessary to salvation. All useful work seemed a vanity, all physical misfortunes were looked upon as punishments, and the darkest of all nights, ignorance and insensibility, lay upon the heart-starved world.

Such was the age out of whose harsh environment the genius of Swedenborg grew, and whose fettering dogmas he was destined to shatter, as the giant trees in the tale burst their bonds. When such a thinker is "let loose upon the world," it is of special interest to recall some of the historic events and personalities centred round his own time.

Swedenborg was born not long after the death of John Amos Comenius, the heroic champion who dealt the first effectual blow at the giant of scholasticism that had for so long a time stalked through the Old World. The year of Swedenborg's birth,

1688, was the year of the fateful though bloodless revolution in England. He lived during the most magnificent part of the reign of Louis XIV, and the memory of La Rochelle was still raw and bitter in the minds of all Protestants. He witnessed the astonishing expeditions of Charles the Mad of Sweden. He was a contemporary of Linnæus. During his last years, Rousseau in France preached his great doctrine of education according to nature, and Diderot developed his philosophy of senses and declared to the world that the blind could be taught. Perhaps no man was ever so precariously situated between traditions of a crumbling civilization and the sudden onrush of a new age toward which his forward-looking mind yearned. The more I consider his position, the less I can see how we are to account for him, except as a miracle, so little did he have in common with his church or the standards of his century. I have not been able to discover anything about the circumstances of his birth and early training which seems to explain the most independent movement ever started in the history of religious thought. Thousands of others have been born of devout parents and admirably educated just as he was, and they have not contributed a new thought or increased the happiness of mankind! But then, is not it ever thus with genius—an angel entertained by us unawares?

Swedenborg's home was in Stockholm, Sweden.

His parents were earnest people. His father was a Lutheran bishop, a professor in the theological seminary and a man of spiritual insight. It is known that Martin Luther, in his monkish days, saw spirits and heard their voices, and many of his followers observed severe fasts and vigils so that they, too, might have glimpses of another world. It is said that the boy Emanuel had some such experiences. In later life he wrote to a friend: "From my fourth to my tenth year I was constantly engaged in thought upon God, salvation and the spiritual experiences of men; and several times I revealed things at which my father and mother wondered, saying that angels must be speaking through me." Though the father may have been sympathetic, his mother interposed with decision and told her husband he "must stop all such celestial excursions," and Emanuel did not see a light or hear a sound from the spiritual world until he was fifty-six years old. From all his religious writings it is clear that he had no use for that kind of experience for children or for unfit men and women. Of all men he was in a position to realize the danger of seeking visions, and he frequently warns his readers against this most harmful practice.

His childhood was as beautiful a beginning as could be desired for a marvellous life. He and his father were constant companions. They climbed the hills around Stockholm and explored the fjords, collecting mosses, flowers and brightly coloured stones. When they returned, the child wrote long reports of their outdoor experiences. For he was a scholar from a child, and his mind always outran the limits of his body. But, unlike many precocious young people, he grew strong and healthy, and his noble, manly bearing was much commented upon.

He received the best education the age and his country afforded. He attended the University of Upsala, and it is said that his earliest productions display much poetical talent. But he devoted himself chiefly to mathematics and mechanics. He surprised his instructors by simplifying some most difficult processes in calculus, and often they could hardly follow his swift mind as it threaded the mazes of learning. They regarded him with awe, and the students spoke of him in low tones. It seems he was an unconscious mirror of the strait-laced tenets and solemn ways amid which he was brought up. His face was described as stern, though not forbidding. He was rather statuesque, but very handsome and commanding in his personality. He was never known to unbend to the gayeties and sports of youth, he could not even in later life make love to the shy young girl who inspired the only passion he ever knew. He went to her father, the distinguished Polheim, instead of to her, and would have proved his love as if by means of charts and

diagrams. The father was willing, and gave the
young man a warrant for the girl returnable in
three years, but the girl was so frightened that her
brother finally persuaded Swedenborg to give her
up. But his love for her he never surrendered.

He graduated from the University of Upsala
with honours, receiving the degree of Doctor of
Philosophy in 1709, when he was twenty-one years
of age. Afterward he travelled in foreign countries,
not for pleasure but to learn. Robsahm in his
*Memoirs* says of Swedenborg, "Of foreign languages, in addition to the learned languages, he
understood well French, English, Dutch, German,
and Italian, for he had journeyed several times in
these countries."

His father wished him to enter the diplomatic
service, but he chose instead the paths of science.
He was given letters of introduction to the sover-
eigns of Europe, but he calmly ignored them and
sought out the most distinguished scholars of his
day. Sometimes he would call unannounced—and
ask for an interview! However, there was something about him which inspired their respect, and
they never declined his request. His one desire,
his mission, was to know, and he levied tribute
upon every one who had new ideas or methods or
processes to impart.

His profound learning brought him into close
association with Christopher Polheim, who seems

to have enjoyed the entire confidence of Charles XII of Sweden. In this way Swedenborg was introduced to the King who in 1716 appointed him assayer in the Swedish College of Mines, that is, an official who gives advice as to the best methods of working mines and smelting ores. With this appointment Swedenborg entered upon a period of amazingly prodigious and diversified activity. Not only did he discharge the duties of his office faithfully and with wisdom, but he also pursued his studies in every department of science. As an independent thinker, he followed the urge of a powerful and original genius to discover, if possible, the deepest secrets of nature. He was as familiar with forge and quarry, workshop and shipyard, as he was with the stars and songs of birds in the morning. The flowers he found blooming in obscure nooks spoke to him secrets as marvellous as those of the majestic mountains he trod. His was a rare blending of the practical and the beautiful, mathematics and poetry, invention and literary power.

In 1718 he turned his mechanical skill to account at the siege of Frederickshall when he constructed machines by which to transport several large vessels a distance of fourteen miles overland, across hills and valleys. He worked on plans for a mechanical carriage, very complicated inside, for a flying carriage, and for a vessel to travel under the sea, thus foreshadowing the automobile, the aëroplane, and the submarine. He worked on plans for new machines for condensing and exhausting air by means of water. He tried to produce a universal musical instrument on which one quite unacquainted with music might execute all kinds of airs that are marked on paper with notes, and he contrived a way of ascertaining the desires and affections of men by analysis.

He devised an air gun capable of discharging a thousand bullets a minute! He had plans for drawbridges, and various other mechanical devices. In him was prefigured the wonderful system of interrelated sciences and arts to which we owe the extraordinary progress of modern times. He showed how the decimal system could be of practical use. He caught marvellous glimpses of knowledge and theories that would be developed a century and a half later—palæontology, biology, mercurial magnetism; he outlined the atomic theory and the nebular hypothesis years in advance of Laplace.

Swedenborg was not blind to the great wealth and influence which these manifold attainments and abilities would bring within his reach. But he refused the cup of happiness lifted to his lips. The sorrows and oppression of mankind lay heavy upon his heart. Humbled, shamed in his soul, he beheld the cruelties of a theology that rained damnation upon myriads of human beings. Jonathan Edwards at the same time in New England preached hell-fire and fear, and countless babies that died without repentance were consigned to everlasting torment! We moderns cannot conceive how the ingenuity of evil was exerted to turn God's Word into a curse. Heaven was monstrous, hell unspeakable, and life one long misery. Swedenborg said to himself, "What is the use of all the knowledge I have gained when such a hideous shadow lies vast across the world?" He turned away from the splendours of fame and spent twenty-nine years—one third of his life—in comparative poverty, comforting the hurt souls of his fellow men with a humane, reasonable doctrine of faith and life.

Besides all his other labour, he wrote every spare hour he could crowd in, and he produced altogether some sixty books and pamphlets before the beginning of his inquiries in the field of religion. Among the great works of this period were "The First Principles of Natural Things," "The Brain," "The Economy of the Animal Kingdom," and "Rational Psychology."

Speaking of those scientific productions, Emerson says: "It seems that he anticipated much of the science of the Nineteenth Century. . . . His writings would be a sufficient library to a lonely and athletic student; and 'The Economy of the Animal Kingdom' is one of those books which, by the sus-

tained dignity of thinking, is an honour to the human
race. The 'Animal Kingdom' is a book of wonderful merits. It was written with the highest end—to
put science and the soul, long estranged from each
other, at one again. It was an anatomist's account
of the human body in the highest style of poetry.
Nothing can exceed the bold and brilliant treat-
ment of a subject usually so dry and repulsive."

Elbert Hubbard says of the "First Principles of
Natural Things" that Darwin seems to have read it
with the most minute care. At any rate, Swedenborg divined something of evolution when he saw
in a tiny lichen on a rock the beginning of a forest.
He also waived the literal account of creation in
the Bible as a contradiction of scientific facts. It
should be added that he never in any of his religious writings changed his attitude toward Genesis.
In fact, he ridiculed and tore down the time-
honoured shrine of literalism, and at the same time
discovered in Scripture what he called a most ancient style of narrative that had nothing at all to
do with the physical creation, but was a long-for-
gotten parable of man's soul.

Besides mathematics, mechanics, and mining,
Swedenborg shows in his works an intimate knowledge of chemistry, anatomy, geology, and a fond-
ness for music. His philosophical subjects were
almost equally varied and extensive. Yet he always
had time "to render himself in all things useful to

society." For many years he was a member of the
Swedish Congress, and on account of his distinguished services to his country he was highly honoured. Many distinctions were conferred upon him
as time passed. In 1724 the Consistory of the University of Upsala invited him to accept a position
as professor of pure mathematics; but he declined.
He was admitted a member of several institutions
of learning, in St. Petersburg, Upsala, and Stockholm. His portrait is in the hall of the Royal
Academy of Sciences at Stockholm, as one of its
distinguished members, hanging near that of
Linnæus.

Swedenborg's life, in a word, seems to have been
nothing but work, work, always work. He became
financially independent, but this only spurred him
on to accomplish more. All persons of high and
low rank bore testimony to his noble character and
selfless devotion. As he grew older, his kind ways
endeared him to all his intimate friends, and the
sternness which characterized his young manhood
melted away. But real companionship he never
knew. He had climbed too high on the ladder of
thought even for his fellow-scientists to converse
with him on some of the subjects with which he was
familiar. They did not attempt to read his works,
but preferred to recommend them. No one seemed
able or willing to follow his giant strides into the
upper realm of speculation. He was an eye among

the blind, an ear among the deaf, a voice crying in
the wilderness with a language they could not
understand. Possibly my own partial isolation from
the world of light and sound gives me this keen
sense of his peculiar situation. But I cannot help
thinking he was lonely with more than earthly loneliness, and the world seemed strange to him because he had already outgrown it. Perhaps no one
had ever endured such a pressure of soul against
the prison bars of flesh as he did, and there was no
reassuring nearness of equal intelligences to lighten
his burden. He had given his life to learn, and what
could he do with his colossal treasure of knowledge? He was naturally glad when more of light,
more opportunity was let into his difficult days;
but I question whether he ever felt quite at home
upon earth after his "illumination."

In about the year 1744 a great change came to
Swedenborg. This keen observer of natural facts
and analyser of things of the mind was given from
on high powers of observation of things spiritual;
the senses of his spirit were quickened to recognize
realities in the spiritual world. His contemporary,
Robsahm, records a conversation in which he asked
Swedenborg "where and how it was granted him
to see and to hear what takes place in the world of
spirits, in heaven, and in hell." The answer was
that in the night one had come to him and said
"that He was the Lord God, the Creator of the

world, and the Redeemer, and that He had chosen me to explain to men the spiritual sense of the Scripture, and that He Himself would explain to me what I should write on this subject; that same night were opened to me, so that I became thoroughly convinced of their reality, the world of spirits, heaven and hell, and I recognized there many acquaintances of every condition in life. From that day I gave up the study of all worldly science, and laboured in spiritual things, according as the Lord had commanded me to write. Afterward the Lord opened, daily very often, my eyes so that in the middle of the day I could see into the other world, and in a state of perfect wakefulness converse with angels and spirits." In September of 1766, Swedenborg wrote to C. F. Oetinger, "I can solemnly bear witness that the Lord Himself has appeared to me, and that He has sent me to do that which I am doing now, and that for this purpose He has opened the interiors of my mind, which are those of my spirit, so that I may see those things which are in the spiritual world and hear those who are there, and which privilege I have had now for twenty-two years." This privileged intercourse continued to the date of his death on March 29, 1772, while temporarily resident in London.

In considering this phase of Swedenborg's experience, I feel that I am peculiarly able to grasp his meaning at least partially. For nearly six years I had no concepts whatever of nature or mind or death or God. I literally thought with my body. Without a single exception my memories of that time are tactual. For thirty years I have examined and re-examined that phase of my development in the light of new theories, and I am convinced of the correctness of what I am saying. I know I was impelled like an animal to seek food and warmth. I remember crying, but not the grief that caused the tears; I kicked, and because I recall it physically, I know I was angry. I imitated those about me when I made signs for things I wanted to eat, or helped to find eggs in my mother's farmyard. But there is not one spark of emotion or rational thought in these distinct yet corporal memories. I was like an unconscious clod of earth. Then, suddenly, I knew not how or where or when, my brain felt the impact of another mind, and I awoke to language, to knowledge, to love, to the usual concepts of nature, of good and evil! I was actually lifted from nothingness to human life—two planes as irreconcilable as Swedenborg's earth experience and his contacts with a realm beyond the cognizance of our physical senses! Since I did not receive even the lowest concepts in those empty years from myself or from nature, I look upon them as a revelation, even if only from a finite mind. Swedenborg looked upon his highest concepts as a revelation from the Infinite Mind. In fact, from his own words it is clear he did not regard his conscious presence in the spiritual world as an end, but as a means of developing the other half of his understanding which as a rule is dormant in us, and seeing more comprehensively different kinds of concepts of good and evil, of spirit and matter, and translating the Word into principles instead of mere words and phrases. He did not say he was the only person who had had that kind of vision. Far from it. What he did say was, he lived twenty-nine years in full consciousness of the real world where all men live at the same time they inhabit the earth. He believed it was his mission to search out and interpret the "spiritual sense," or sacred symbolism, of the Scriptures, and that his experiences in the other world were to help him to understand truly the Word of God, and convey the most wonderful and beneficent truths to mankind. Therefore Swedenborg devoted himself with all his former energy and courage to the investigation of the facts and laws of the soul realm. He took up the study of Hebrew, so that he might read the Old Testament in the original language and gain a first-hand knowledge of the religious forms and parables and "mysteries" of ancient times. It is evident that for many years he had endeavoured to grasp the meaning of countless obscure passages in the Word, and had constantly felt baffled! Many things had troubled him, tradition and the almost unconquerable habit of sectarian interpretation, the coldness of an age that left out of Christianity its very heart of love, the witchcraft of a church literature ably and brilliantly advocating tenets that were never dreamed of by any prophet or Apostle, and finally the obsessing illusions of the senses. But at last the light broke upon his mind—the Truth made him free—and he gave all his magnificent powers to the release of the world!

In 1747, Swedenborg asked and obtained leave of Frederic, then King of Sweden, to retire from the office of assessor, so that he might not be disturbed in his new work. A higher degree of rank was offered him, but he refused, fearing that it might be an occasion of inspiring him with pride. Thus he withdrew quietly from the splendours of a notable society and the honours that had crowned him to the seclusion of his little library, where he produced twenty-seven books, the sole object of which was to make Christianity a living reality upon earth.

Whatever may be the opinions of those who read Swedenborg's religious books, one cannot but be impressed by his unique personality. He did everything gently and deliberately. There was nothing of excitement or elation about him. The farther he travelled in the spiritual realm, the more humble and composed he became. He refused to appeal to the weakness or credulity of the ignorant. He did not attempt to make any proselytes; nor did he wish to have his name connected with the New Church

which he said the Lord was about to establish in the
world. He felt that his message was for posterity
rather than for his generation; and as his works—
the result of long, hard years of labour—left the
press in large Latin folios, he distributed them free
among the universities and the clergy of Europe.
Walt Whitman says that "we convince by our presences," and that is powerfully true of the Swedish
seer as he worked at his colossal task. He fully realized the incredulity and hostility with which many of
his statements would be viewed, and he could have
rendered them more attractive by omitting or soften-
ing down unpleasant truths in a charming and enter-
taining manner. Yet he never flinched or turned aside
from his high trust. When he passed out of the body
which had become so painfully inadequate to his
soaring mind, a degree of obloquy fell upon his illus-
trious name; and for a time one of the noblest cham-
pions true Christianity has ever known was nearly
forgotten. The only reward he ever knew in his growing isolation upon earth was the consciousness that
he was giving his full measure of devotion to the
welfare and happiness of all men. There are some
lines by John Drinkwater in his "Lincoln" which
always bring Swedenborg vividly before me:

"Lonely is the man who understands.
Lonely is vision that leads a man away
From the pasture-lands,
From the furrows of corn and the brown loads of hay

To the mountain-side,
To the high places where contemplation brings
All his adventurings
Among the sowers and the tillers in the wide
Valleys to one fused experience,
That shall control
The course of his soul,
And give his hand
Courage and continence."

Yes, with matchless constancy the seer possessed
his soul in loneliness and vision!

A hundred and fifty-five years have passed since
Swedenborg's death, and slowly his achievements
have been winning recognition. The antagonism
which his doctrines once aroused has changed to an
attitude of tolerance and inquiry. Many intelligent
people have advocated his teachings in the centres of
civilization and carried them to nooks and corners of
the world undreamed of by most of us. His message
has travelled like light, side by side with the new
science, the new freedom, and the new society, which
are struggling to realize themselves in the life of mankind. I keep coming across instances of handicapped
or disappointed lives which have been enriched and
brightened by that Great Message. I, too, have my
humble testimony, and I shall be most happy if
through a word of mine even one individual gains a
sweeter sense of God's presence or a keener zest
for mastering the difficulties of outward environment.

As I wander through the dark, encountering difficulties, I am aware of encouraging voices that murmur from the spirit realm. I sense a holy passion pouring down from the springs of Infinity. I thrill to music that beats with the pulses of God. Bound to suns and planets by invisible cords, I feel the flame of eternity in my soul. Here, in the midst of the every-day air, I sense the rush of ethereal rains. I am conscious of the splendour that binds all things of earth to all things of heaven—immured by silence and darkness, I possess the light which shall give me vision a thousandfold when death sets me free.

## II

MY IMPRESSIONS of my first contact with the writings of the great Swedish seer of the Eighteenth Century, which came about thirty years ago, will seem without meaning unless I go back to my first questionings about God. As a little child I naturally wanted to know who made everything in the world and I was told that Nature (they called it Mother Nature) had made earth and sky and water and all living creatures. This satisfied me for a time, and I was happy among the rose-trees of my mother's garden, or on the bank of a river, or out in the daisy-pranked fields, where my teacher told me true "Arabian Nights" tales about seeds and flowers, birds and insects and the fishes in the river. Like other children, I believed that every object I touched was alive and self-conscious, and I supposed we were all Mother Nature's children. But as I grew older, I began to reason about the parts of Nature I could touch. Obviously, I am using mature words and the ideas of later years to make intelligible the groping, half-formed, ever-shifting impressions of childhood. I noticed a difference between the way human beings did their work and the way the wonders of Nature were wrought. I saw that puppies, flowers, stones, babies, and thunderstorms were not just put together as my mother mixed her hot cakes. There was an order and sequence of things in field and wood that puzzled me, and at the same time there was a confusion in the elements which at times terrified me. The wanton destruction of the beautiful and the ugly, the useful and the obnoxious, the righteous and the wicked by earthquake or flood or tornado I could not understand. How could such a blind mass of irresponsible forces create and keep alive, always renewing what was destroyed, and keep up an unfailing succession of spring, summer, autumn, and winter, seedtime and harvest, day and night, tides and generations of men? Somehow I sensed that Nature was no more concerned with me or those I loved than with a twig or a fly, and this awoke in me something akin to resentment—"the fine innuendo by which the Soul makes its enormous claim," and declares that it has a prerogative of control over the course of events and things.

Turning away from Nature, I inquired about God, and again I was baffled. Friends tried to tell me He was the Creator, and that He was everywhere, that He knew all the needs, joys, and sorrows of every human life, and nothing happened without His foreknowledge and providence. Some with a generous disposition said He was merciful to all, and caused His sun to shine on the just and the unjust alike. I was drawn irresistibly to such a glorious, lovable Being, and I longed really to understand something

about Him. Then I met Phillips Brooks, and he
helped me, with his simple soul-stirring words, to
grasp the central truth that God is Love, and that
His Love is the "Light of all men."

But I could not form any clear idea of the relation
between this Divine Love and the material world. I
lost myself many times in shadows and uncertainties,
wandering back and forth between the Light which
was so ineffably reassuring and the chaos and darkness of nature that seemed so real as not to be gain-
said. One day I was made radiantly happy and
brought nearer to a sense of God when "I watched"
an exquisite butterfly, just out of its cocoon, dry-
ing its wings in the sun, and afterward felt it flutter-
ing over a bunch of trailing arbutus. Someone told
me how the ancient Egyptians had looked upon the
butterfly as an emblem of immortality. I was de-
lighted. It seemed to me as it should be, that such
beautiful forms of life should have in them a lesson
about things still more lovely. Nevertheless, the same
buzz-saw continued to worry me until one day a sudden flash of intuition revealed an infinite wonder to
me.

I had been sitting quietly in the library for half an
hour. I turned to my teacher and said, "Such a
strange thing has happened! I have been far away all
this time, and I haven't left the room." "What do you
mean, Helen?" she asked, surprised. "Why," I cried,
"I have been in Athens." Scarcely were the words

out of my mouth when a bright, amazing realization
seemed to catch my mind and set it ablaze. I perceived the realness of my soul and its sheer inde-
pendence of all conditions of place and body. It
was clear to me that it was because I was a spirit
that I had so vividly "seen" and felt a place thousands of miles away. Space was nothing to spirit! In
that new consciousness shone the Presence of God,
Himself a Spirit everywhere at once, the Creator
dwelling in all the universe simultaneously. The fact
that my little soul could reach out over continents
and seas to Greece, despite a blind, deaf, and stum-
bling body, sent another exulting emotion rushing
over me. I had broken through my limitations and
found in touch an eye. I could read the thoughts of
wise men—thoughts which had for ages survived
their mortal life, and could possess them as part of
myself. If this were true, how much more could
God, the uncircumscribed Spirit, cancel the harms
of nature—accident, pain, destruction, and reach out
to his children. Deafness and blindness, then, were
of no real account. They were to be relegated to the
outer circle of my life. Of course I did not sense any
such process with my child-mind; but I did know
that I, the real I, could leave the library and visit
any place I wanted to, mentally, and I was happy.
That was the little seed from which grew my interest
in spiritual subjects.

I was not at that time especially enthusiastic

about the Bible stories, except the story of the gentle Nazarene. The accounts of creation and the driving out of Adam and Eve from Eden for eating a particular fruit, the Flood and all the wrath and vengeance of the Lord seemed to me very similar to the Greek and Roman myths I had read—and there were very few gods and goddesses I could admire.

I was disappointed not to find in the Bible that my good aunt held up to me as a Divine Book, a likeness of the Being whose face shone so benign, beautiful, and radiant in my heart. She told me tales out of the Apocalypse, and still I felt a void I could not explain. What could I see in a war between God and dragons and horned beasts? How could I associate the eternal torture of those cast into the lake of fire with the God whom Christ declared to be love? Why, I wondered, should one particular City of God be described with pavements of gold and walls of precious stones when heaven must be full of everything else just as magnificent—mountains, fields, oceans, and the sweet, fruitful earth, restful to the feet? The touching story of Christ, comforting the sorrowful, healing the sick, giving new light to the blind and speech to mute lips stirred me to the depths; but how could I worship three persons—the Father, the Son, and the Holy Ghost? Was that not the sort of false worship so terribly punished in Old Testament days?

Such were the bewildered, dissatisfied thoughts on

the Bible which possessed my mind when there came into my life one of the friends I loved most, Mr. John Hitz, who had for a long period held the position at Washington of Consul-General for Switzerland in this country. Afterward he was superintendent of the Volta Bureau in Washington, which Dr. Bell founded with the Volta Prize money he received for inventing the telephone. This bureau was established for the purpose of collecting and distributing information about the deaf, and publishing a magazine in their behalf, which is now called *The Volta Review*.

I met Mr. Hitz first in 1893, when I was about thirteen years old, and that was the beginning of an affectionate and beautiful friendship which I cherish among the dearest memories of my life. He was always deeply interested in all I did—my studies, my girlish joys and dreams, my struggle through college and my work for the blind. He was one of the few who fully appreciated my teacher and the peculiar significance of her work not only to me, but to all the world. His letters bore testimony to his affection for her and his understanding of what she was to me—a light in all dark places. He visited us often in Boston and Cambridge, and every time my teacher and I stopped over in Washington on our way to or from my southern home, we had delightful trips with him.

After my teacher and I settled down in Wrentham, Mass., he spent six weeks with us every summer until the year before he died. He loved to take me out walking early in the morning while the dew lay upon grass and tree and the air was joyous with bird-songs. We wandered through still woods, fragrant meadows, past the picturesque stone walls of Wrentham, and always he brought me closer to the beauty and the deep meaning of Nature. As he talked, the great world shone for me in the glory of immortality. He stimulated in me the love of Nature that is so precious a part of the music in my silence and the light in my darkness. It is sweet as I write to recall the flowers and the laughing brooks and the shining, balmy moments of stillness in which we had joy together. Each day I beheld through his eyes a new and charming landscape, "wrapped in exquisite showers" of fancy and spiritual beauty. We would often pause that I might feel the swaying of the trees, the bending of the flowers, and the waving of the corn, and he would say, "the wind that puts all this life into Nature is a marvellous symbol of the spirit of God."

On my fourteenth birthday he presented me with a gold watch he had worn for more than thirty years, and I have never been separated from it since, except one time when it was sent to Switzerland for some parts that were worn out. Curiously enough, it was not made for the blind in the first place. It once belonged to a German ambassador who had it fixed so that he could keep important appointments exactly. He was obliged to call upon a high dignitary of the Kaiser, and it was not etiquette to look at the watch, nor was it etiquette to stay too long. So the Ambassador went to a jeweller and gave him instructions about making the watch so that he could slip his hand into his pocket and "feel" the time. It has a crystal face, and a gold hand on the back, which is connected with the minute hand, and goes with it and stops with it. There are also gold points around the rim of the watch which indicate the hours. I wear it always against my heart, and it ticks for me as faithfully as my friend himself worked for me and loved me. He whose love it keeps ever before me has been gone nearly twenty years, but I have the sweet consciousness that each tick is bringing me nearer and nearer to him. Truly a treasure above price, linking time and eternity!

Mr. Hitz and I corresponded for many years. He learned the Braille system so that I could read myself his long and frequent letters. These letters are a record of spiritual kinship which it comforts me to read over when I long for the touch of his hand and the wise, inspiring words with which he encouraged me in my tasks. His first and last thought was how to lessen the obstacles I encountered. He quickly perceived my hunger for books I could read on subjects that particularly interested me, and how limited were the embossed books within my reach. For eight years he devoted a part of each day to copying whatever he thought would give me pleasure—stories, biographies of great men, poetry, and studies of Nature. When, after reading "Heaven and Hell," I expressed a wish to know more of Swedenborg's writings, he laboriously compiled books of explanations and extracts to facilitate my reading. All this he accomplished in addition to his duties as superintendent of the Volta Bureau and his extensive correspondence! In his letters he often referred to "the quiet morning hours before breakfast" he spent transcribing for me, and his "joy of being in daily touch with his *innigst geliebte Tochter Helena.*" Many friends have done wonderful things for me, but nothing like Mr. Hitz's untiring effort to share with me the inner sunshine and peace which filled his silent years. Each year I was drawn closer to him, and he wrote to me more constantly as the days passed. Then came a great sorrow—separation from the friend I loved best next to my teacher. I had been visiting my mother, and was on my way back to Wrentham. As usual, I stopped in Washington, and Mr. Hitz came to the train to meet me. He was full of joy as he embraced me, saying how impatiently he had awaited my coming. Then, as he was leading me from the train, he had a sudden attack of heart trouble, and passed away. Just before the end he took my hand, and I still feel his pressure when I think of that dark time. I could not have borne the loss of such an intimate and tender friend if I had thought he was indeed dead. But his noble philosophy and certainty of the life to come braced me with an unwavering faith that we should meet again in a world happier and more beautiful than anything of my dreaming. With me remains always the helpful memory of his rare personality.

He was a man of lofty character, a man of rich spiritual gifts. His heart was pure and warm, full of childlike faith in the best he saw in his fellow-creatures, and he was always doing for other people something lovely and dear. In all his ways he kept the Commandment, "Love thy neighbour as thyself." At eighty years of age he had the heart of an evergreen, and his inexhaustible power of enjoyment lifted him far above the average of humanity. He remained young with the young. He was never old to me, and I was never deaf and blind to him. He spelled with difficulty on his fingers, and he was so hard of hearing I had often to repeat a sentence six times with my imperfect speech before he could understand me. But our love covered a multitude of difficulties, and our intercourse was always worth every effort it cost us.

As we talked thus, Mr. Hitz came to realize fully my hunger for literature I could read on subjects that especially interested me. He himself had grown deaf, and that enabled him to see the distorted angle of my thoughts with regard to the world of the senses. He told me that if I would only try to put my-

self in the place of those with sight and hearing and
divine their impressions of things, they could unite
their senses with mine more and more and thus
wonderfully increase my enjoyment of the outer
world. He showed me how I could find a key to their
life, and give them a chance to explore my own with
understanding. He put into my hands a copy of
Swedenborg's "Heaven and Hell" in raised letters.
He said he knew I would not understand much of it
at first, but it was fine exercise for my mind, and
would satisfy me with a likeness of a God as lovable
as the one in my heart. He told me always to remember that it is easier to see what is good than
what is true in a difficult book. For, as Swedenborg
put it, "Good is like a little flame which gives light,
and causes man to see, perceive, and believe."

When I began "Heaven and Hell" I was as little
aware of the new joy coming into my life as I had
been years before when I stood on the piazza steps
awaiting my teacher. Impelled only by the curiosity
of a young girl who loves to read, I opened that big
book, and lo, my fingers lighted upon a paragraph in
the preface about a blind woman whose darkness
was illumined with beautiful truths from Swedenborg's writings. She believed that they imparted a
light to her mind which more than compensated her
for the loss of earthly light. She never doubted that
there was a spiritual body within the material one
with perfect senses, and that after a few dark years

the eyes within her eyes would open to a world infinitely more wonderful, complete, and satisfying than this. My heart gave a joyous bound. Here was a faith that emphasized what I felt so keenly—the separateness between soul and body, between a realm I could picture as a whole and the chaos of fragmentary things and irrational contingencies which my limited physical senses met at every turn. I let myself go, as healthy, happy youth will, and tried to puzzle out the long words and the weighty thoughts of the Swedish sage. Somehow I sensed the likeness of Him whom I loved as the One and Only, and I wanted to understand more. The words Love and Wisdom seemed to caress my fingers from paragraph to paragraph, and these two words released in me new forces to stimulate my somewhat indolent nature and urge me forward evermore. I came back to the book from time to time, picking up a line here and a line there, "precept upon precept," one glimpse then another of the Divine Word hidden under the clouds of literal statement. As I realized the meaning of what I read, my soul seemed to expand and gain confidence amid the difficulties which beset me. The descriptions of the other world bore me far, far over measureless regions bathed in superhuman beauty and strangeness, where angels' robes flash, where great lives and creative minds cast a splendour upon darkest circumstances, where events and mighty combats sweep by endlessly, where the night is lit to eternal day by the Smile of God. I glowed through and through as I sat in that atmosphere of the soul and watched men and women of nobler mould pass in majestic procession. For the first time immortality put on intelligibility for me, and earth wore new curves of loveliness and significance. I was glad to discover that the City of God was not a stupid affair of glass streets and sapphire walls, but a systematic treasury of wise, helpful thoughts and noble influences. Gradually I came to see that I could use the Bible, which had so baffled me, as an instrument for digging out precious truths, just as I could use my hindered, halting body for the high behests of my spirit.

I had been told by narrow people that all who were not Christians would be punished, and naturally my soul revolted, since I knew of wonderful men who had lived and died for truth as they saw it in the pagan lands. But in "Heaven and Hell" I found that "Jesus" stands for Divine Good, Good wrought into deeds, and "Christ" Divine Truth, sending forth new thought, new life and joy into the minds of men; therefore no one who believes in God and lives right is ever condemned. So I grew to womanhood, and as unaccountably as Conrad found in English the language of his choice, I took more and more to the New Church doctrines as my religion. No one encouraged me in this choice, and I cannot explain it any more than anyone else. I can

only say that the Word of God freed from the blots
and stains of barbarous creeds has been at once the
joy and good of my life, wonderfully linked with my
growing appreciation of my teacher's work and my
own responsibilities of service, hours of struggle and
solitude, hours of deepest joy, harsh truths faced
squarely and high dreams held dearer than the pleasant baits of ease and complaisance. Those truths
have been to my faculties what light, colour, and
music are to the eye and ear. They have lifted my
wistful longing for a fuller sense-life into a vivid
consciousness of the complete being within me. Each
day comes to me with both hands full of possibilities,
and in its brief course I discern all the verities and
realities of my existence, the bliss of growth, the
glory of action, the spirit of beauty.

# III

Do I hear someone say, "But is not deaf and blind Helen Keller liable to be imposed upon by those whose opinions or dogmas or political ideals are confined to a small minority?" Before considering Swedenborg's claims, which have astonished the world ever since they were made, I should like to lay before the reader the opinions of well-known writers who were conversant with his works, but who have had no affiliations with the church which treasures his religious teachings.

It will be remembered that Emerson chose Swedenborg as one of his "Representative Men." He says:

"This man, who appeared to his contemporaries a visionary and elixir of moonbeams, no doubt led the most real life of any man then in the world. . . . A colossal soul, he lies vast abroad on his times, uncomprehended by them, and requires a long focal distance to be seen." It should be noted in passing that Emerson had no eye for Swedenborg's hell or mind for his Bible symbolism.

Thomas Carlyle was a canny Scot not likely to be led astray. This is his estimate of Swedenborg:

"A man of great and indisputable cultivation, strong, mathematical intellect, and the most pious, seraphic turn of mind; a man beautiful, lovable, and tragical to me. . . . More truths are confessed in his writings than in those of any other man. . . . One of the loftiest minds in the realm of mind. . . . One of the spiritual suns that will shine brighter as the years go on."

Elbert Hubbard's comparison between Swedenborg and Shakespeare is of special interest, as he approaches the subject from an entirely different mental angle:

"They are Titans both. In the presence of such giants, small men seem to wither and blow away. Swedenborg was cast in heroic mould, and no man since history began ever compassed in himself so much physical science, and, with it all on his back, made such daring voyages into the clouds. The men who soar highest and know most about another world usually know little about this. No man of his time was so competent a scientist as Swedenborg, and no man before or since has mapped so minutely the Heavenly Kingdom.

"Shakespeare's feet were never really off the ground. His excursion in 'The Tempest' was only in a captured balloon. Ariel and Caliban he secured out of an old book of fables.

"Shakespeare knew little about physics; economics and sociology never troubled him; he had small Latin and less Greek; he never travelled, and the history of the rocks was to him a blank.

"Swedenborg anticipated Darwin in a dozen ways; he knew the classic languages and most of the modern; he travelled everywhere; he was a practical economist, and the best civil engineer of his day."

Henry James said: "Emanuel Swedenborg had the sanest and most far-reaching intellect this age has known," and Henry Ward Beecher was no less sweeping in his assertion, "No one can know the theology of the Nineteenth Century who has not read Swedenborg."

There are others who bear interesting witness to the impression left upon them by Swedenborg's teachings. Among them was Elizabeth Barrett Browning, whose beauty of soul and exquisite poetry excited such admiration everywhere. "To my mind," she says, "the only light that has been cast on the other life is found in Swedenborg's philosophy. It explains much that was incomprehensible."

Samuel Taylor Coleridge, whom the Encyclopædia Britannica notes as "one of the most remarkable poets and thinkers," pays this tribute to one who has been hastily called by some a madman:

"I can venture to assert, as a moralist, Swedenborg is above all praise; and that, as a naturalist, psychologist, and theologian, he has strong and varied claims on the gratitude and admiration of the professional and philosophical faculties. . . . Thrice happy should we be if the learned teachers of to-day were gifted with a like madness!"

Such estimates by these distinguished men and women are helpful in forming some idea of the personality and commanding genius Swedenborg possessed. Any defect there may be in my own judgment of him is evidently not due to my physical limitations. Measured by those who are scholars themselves, and others who are esteemed for spiritual gifts, he is proclaimed to have had an amazingly well-trained intellect—trained, as Emerson observes, "to work with astronomic precision." If he had been an illiterate man, no matter how wonderful his experience, and how authentic his claims, he could not long have stood his ground before the pitiless battery of competent inquiry. But here is a scholar far ahead of his time, mastering the arts and sciences, writing able and voluminous works on every wonder of Nature from the tiny lichen on the rocks to the most complex structure of the brain, always preserving a splendid balance on dizzy heights of learning where he must needs climb alone; and then with the same audacity, calmness, and composure, feeling his perilous way over the deeps and abysses of the spirit-world and revealing with fearless authority the delicate yet unbreakable links between mind and matter, eternity and time, God and man.

Three of my dear friends have had something to say, and they would not have said it of a lunatic or an intolerant fanatic. I knew Dr. Edward Everett Hale longest, and I always marvelled at his freshness of interest in all things and the variety of subjects upon which he deeply pondered. It was he who passed this judgment:

"Swedenborgianism has done the liberating work of the last century. The wave Swedenborg started lasts to this day. The statements of his religious works have revolutionized theology."

Like all who loved Bishop Brooks, I realize what weight and significance his public utterances carry with them. His opinion of this subject is surely deserving of consideration:

"I have the profoundest honour for the character and work of Emanuel Swedenborg. . . . I have from time to time gained much from his writings. It is impossible to say a little on so great a theme. Yes, in a true sense, we are all New Churchmen, with new light, new hopes, and new communion with God in Christ."

And Whittier, the dear, mystic poet, said, "There is one grand and beautiful idea underlying all his revelations about the future life."

Another way to appreciate Swedenborg, the man, is to compare him with other great world leaders. There is a story out of ancient times that a king left his council chamber weary and disheartened. He called for Iliff the artist and commanded: "Paint me a true man's picture, gracious and wise, endowed with the strength of heroes and the beauty of womanhood. It shall hang in my inmost chamber, and when I retire thither, it shall fill my soul with grandeur and warm it with sacred fire." The picture was painted and hung in the palace hall. The king gazed on it with rapt delight, until suddenly he discerned a strange meaning that puzzled him. The form was that of his most graceful courtier, perfect in every line! The bearing was that of the humble attendant who filled the cup for him; the brow was that of a priest in holy vision; the eye was that of the wandering minstrel who charmed his tired spirit with song. The smile was that of his wife, so sweet and constant. Thus was the picture graced with all their charms, and they also were glorified in a new light. So the picture of Swedenborg seems to gather unto itself gleams of nobility from the lives of many great men, and they also gain a new significance from the comparison. In science, literature, and philosophy there are those who stand like heralds on mountain-tops proclaiming a new day, of which they catch the first rays. There are patriots who deliver their country from a cruel yoke or lead the people to a truer freedom. There are those who search the treasuries of earth and discover new stores of light and heat; there are those who reveal countless stars and distant planets, and still others who sail many seas and find—not a Northwest Passage, but an America. Finally, in religion there are leaders who teach millions by example or precept, who destroy idolatry or who awaken the temple or church from superstitions and hypocrisy; and again others, like Wesley, who pour love into the coldness of an un-spiritual age.

So one impressive figure after another appears on the screen of imagination when we contemplate Swedenborg. There is Michaelangelo who saw an angel in the stone and "carved it with a sharp inci-sion until he caught the vision." But Swedenborg's inner eyes were opened to behold living angels, and out of the literal truths of the Word of God, which are its stones, he carved heavenly messages of love and help from God to His children.

Another touch is given to the picture when we think of Beethoven, Mozart, and Wagner, pouring into the world harmonies that lifted men's hearts to heaven, while Swedenborg perceived the divine har-mony in the universe, and, as he said, actually heard sweetest music sung by angelic multitudes.

From our childhood we have been familiar with the characters of Napoleon, Wellington, Washington, and Grant, and the fearful battles they took part in. But it was Swedenborg's lot to witness war between the forces of good and evil in the spiritual world; and, armed with the weapons of heaven—the new doctrines of the World—and the sword of earth—the truths of nature—he is the greatest champion of genuine Christianity in twenty centuries.

Alexander I of Russia set the serfs free, and Lin-coln abolished Negro slavery in the United States.

Over the temple of religion Swedenborg saw written, "Now it is permitted to enter intellectually into the mysteries of faith," and he gave mankind a spiritual philosophy which liberated their minds and overthrew the power of ecclesiastical despotism.

What Agassiz did in zoölogy and palæontology, Karl Marx in economics and Darwin in evolution, Swedenborg did in religion. With massive arguments and thundering anathemas he sent a continent's literature of pessimism, condemnation, and insincerity crashing down into the abyss.

Aristotle, Plato, Francis Bacon, and Kant were philosophers of brilliant genius who sought long and patiently for the Causes of all things. Not only has our seer been justly called "the Swedish Aristotle," but he has declared that he was permitted to enter consciously into the very World of Causes and live in its Light for twenty-nine years.

Columbus's undaunted faith was realized in the discovery of a new continent, and Cortez "stood on a peak in Darien" with the Pacific immense upon his vision. Now we have before us an explorer who travelled through the "undiscovered country," heard its language with his ears, conversed with its inhabitants, and described to our world, "from things heard and seen," its life and climate and civilization. For example, in his "Heaven and Hell" he wrote:

"When a man's acts are disclosed to him after

death, the angels to whom is given the office of searching look into his face and the search is extended through the whole body, beginning from the fingers of each hand, and thus proceeding through the whole. Because I wondered as to the reason of this, it was made known to me, namely, that as all things of the thought and will are inscribed on the brain, for their beginnings are there, so also they are inscribed on the whole body; since all the things of thought and will extend thither from their beginnings, and there terminate, as in their ultimates. . . . From these things it may be evident what is meant by the book of man's life, spoken of in the Word, namely this, that all things, both what he has thought and what he has done, are inscribed on the whole man, and appear as if read in a book when they are called forth from the memory, and as if presented to sight when the spirit is viewed in the light of heaven."

Isaac Newton, who was like minded with him in his pure, devout sentiments, was inspired to see the laws of attraction in the physical realm. Swedenborg perceived that love is the corresponding attractive law in the spiritual realm, and he testified that he beheld the radiating source of love actually as a sun, giving life to all souls and beauty to all creation. From his "Divine Love and Wisdom" I will quote one or two extracts to illustrate the facts and laws he calls inner realities:

"That there is any other sun than the sun of the natural world has hitherto been unknown. The reason is, that the spiritual of man has so far passed into his natural, that he does not know what the spiritual is, nor consequently that there is a spiritual world, in which are spirits and angels, other than and different from the natural world. Since the spiritual world has remained so deeply hidden from those who are in the natural world, therefore it has pleased the Lord to open the sight of my spirit, that I might see the things which are in that world, as I see those which are in the natural world, and afterward describe that world, which was done in the work on 'Heaven and Hell,' in one chapter of which the sun of the spiritual world has also been treated of. For it was seen by me, and it appeared of the same size as the sun of the natural world, and also fiery like it, but with a redder glow. And it was made known to me that the universal angelic heaven is under that sun; and that the angels of the third heaven see it always, the angels of the second heaven very often, and the angels of the first or lowest heaven sometimes.

"Since love and fire correspond to each other, the angels cannot see love with their eyes, but instead of love that which corresponds to it. For angels have an internal and an external as well as men; their internal thinks and is wise and wills and loves, and their external feels, sees, speaks,

and acts; and all their externals are correspondences of internals, but spiritual correspondences,
and not natural. Divine Love also is felt as fire
by spiritual beings; and therefore where fire is men-
tioned in the Word, it signifies love. The holy fire
in the Israelitish Church had that signification;
when it is customary in prayers to God, to ask
that heavenly fire, that it, the Divine Love, may
kindle the heart."

"Man in his thought has not penetrated deeper
than to the interior or purer things of Nature; for
which reason also many have placed the dwellings
of angels and spirits in ether, and some in the
stars; thus within Nature and not above or out of it;
when yet angels and spirits are entirely above or
out of Nature, and in their own world, which is under another sun. And because in that world spaces
are appearances, therefore it cannot be said that
they are in the ether or in the stars; for they are
with man, conjoined to the affection and the thought
of his spirit. For a man is a spirit; from that he
thinks and wills; and therefore the spiritual world
is where man is, and not at all removed from him.
In a word, every man as to the interiors of his
mind is in that world, in the midst of angels and
spirits there; and he thinks from its light, and loves
from its heat."

"As regards the sun from which the angels have
light and heat, it appears above the lands on which

the angels dwell, at an elevation of about forty-five degrees, which is the middle altitude; and it also appears distant from the angels as the sun of the world from men. That sun appears always in that altitude and at that distance, nor does it move. Hence it is that the angels have not time divided into days and years, nor any progression of the day from morning through mid-day to evening and into night; not any progression of the year from spring through summer to autumn and into winter; but there is perpetual light and perpetual spring."

Finally, in forming an idea of Swedenborg's place in the life thought of the world, we may recall the religious teachers of mankind. Buddha lived his gentle life which shone as an example before the peoples of the Orient. Confucius taught by precept, Mahomet carried his message of one God with fire and sword through lands given over to idolatry. Swedenborg strove to impart a sane, clear-eyed faith—rational truths that alone can protect religion from ignorance, brute force, and the cunning of those who would use it as a means of oppression. Those other leaders, earnest and sincere as they were, did not possess the science, the perception of human motives, and the militant truths which alone can prevent society from forging fetters for the minds and bodies of men.

Martin Luther protested against the superstitious practices of the Dark Ages, and the Reformation began. Wesley broke down the formality of the English Church, and the enthusiastic service of his followers to humanity is now world-wide. But many of the fundamental teachings remain, and a noble exponent of the Catholic Church, Cardinal Newman, whose "Apologia" I read attentively years ago, laid bare great inconsistencies that ought to be faced squarely by all Protestants. Swedenborg brought to all sects in Christendom an abundance of new truths, he was the Herald of a new dispensation. It is worth while to note the comment of a Roman Catholic theologian, Professor Johann Joseph von Goerres in this connection:

"Throughout the voluminous works of Swedenborg, everything appears simple and uniform, especially as to the tone in which he writes, in which there is no effort at display in the imaginative powers, nothing overwrought, nothing fantastic. . . . In the cultivation of science, sincerity and simplicity of heart are necessary requirements to the attainment of durable success. We never observe that Swedenborg was subject to that pride by the influence of which so many great spirits have fallen; he always remained the same subdued and modest mind; and never, either by success or by any consideration, lost his mental equilibrium."

Whatever opinion may be formed of the nature or the value of Swedenborg's claims, it is obvious that his experience is a unique one. No other man, highly trained in all the sciences of his time, has ever asserted that he was in constant intercourse with another world for more than a quarter of a century, while possessing all his faculties intact. Partial, occasional, even frequent and habitual glimpses of the spirit realm are recorded in every age and everywhere. Moses had visions of God and life. Through him the sacred symbolism of the Jewish dispensation was given, and he understood the importance of leading his people out of slavery to a new civilization; but he did not sense the Divine Message couched in the Word for the human race. The Prophets, also, had visions and heard voices, but Isaiah, Jeremiah, and Daniel were evidently unaware of the higher truths they were conveying to all nations symbolically; most of them saw only the narrower historical meaning of the Message.

The Apostle Paul comprehended many truths of the Word spiritually, and his epistles are more illuminating than all those of the other Apostles put together. He was caught up into the third heaven, but could not tell what he saw. Indeed, he said he did not know whether he was in the body or out of it. These instances were, so to speak, reports of local events in a strange country, while Swedenborg was consciously admitted to that Strange Country, and prepared by long observation to make known the life and laws of heaven, the world of spirits and hell. The Apostle of Love, John, beheld in vision the future state of the Christian world and the glory of a new humanity. What he saw in symbol, Swedenborg saw in reality. He bore witness to the fulfilment of those prophetic pictures, and explained every scene, so that the Apocalypse is no longer a sealed book; it lies open, its seals broken and its message shining with the splendour of the Lord's second coming.

"An incredible claim!" I hear someone exclaim. Yet it seems to me less incredible than the claim that a native of Stratford, with scarcely any classical education and no advantages whatever, should have produced twenty-seven immortal plays. What Emanuel Swedenborg with his "vast, indisputable cultivation" does claim is, that he was the divinely chosen and prepared interpreter of the parables and symbols and other mysteries of the Word, to disclose the influences of another world which we often "feel" so vividly, and gladden the deserts of life with new ideas of will, wisdom, power, and joy. That, he declared, heralded the second coming of the Lord, a coming to man in a doctrine of right living and true thinking. If this seems incredible, it should be remembered that that is what most people say of anything out of the common.

In 1880, certain men knew that flying-machines could be equipped and rendered safe; but few would listen to them because such a thing had never been done. So flying came slowly, and as the achievement of a small, faithful minority, labouring in an atmosphere of ridicule. There are other funds of knowledge building up. We know, for instance, that it is possible so to plan the economic systems in the world that we could all be much richer and freer and happier in producing comforts and pleasures than we are to-day. We know with at least an equal certainty that we can reorganize the whole educational system so that the bulk of mankind will grow up more happily prepared for creative service. We know that the international troubles of our time, the hostilities between peoples, the menace of war, are largely due to mental concepts which can be changed only by suggestion, persistence, training, and sheer devotion to humanity. Yet so-called educated people are incredulous of social, political, and spiritual developments they may live to see and share. The small group of believers who know must struggle on, bearing steadfast witness to their truth in schools, courts, workshops, offices, and legislatures; and what are they but messengers in their way of the Lord's second coming?

World events, too, seem to be full of this immense significance. Nations have become so dependent one upon another for the support of life that war is more than ever madness. External pressure is brought upon mankind to make them see the need of living in peace and brotherhood. About a century ago man found out the use of coal and steam for the manufacture of goods in great quantities, and for transportation by sea and rail. Soon followed the telegraph and the telephone and improved machines of every kind, and now come the radio and the ships that move through the air and under the sea. God has spread around the world three vast girders of coal and iron and electricity which have swept all the peoples into one great brotherhood of work!

"But how can I accept such an audacious and peculiar claim, contrary to everything I have observed?" someone again demands. It is true that when we read the works of other authors we have accepted rules and canons of criticism to guide us; but in the case of Swedenborg we have almost none. From the very nature of such a case we can know little or nothing about the psychological states through which he passed, except what he himself reports. His own testimony must convince us, if anything can.

That is nothing new to my experience. Daily I place implicit faith in my friends with eyes and ears, and they tell me how often their senses deceive and lead them astray. Yet out of their evidence I gather countless precious truths with which I build my world, and my soul is enabled to picture the beauty of the sky and listen to the songs of birds. All about me may be silence and darkness, yet within me, in the spirit, is music and brightness, and colour flashes through all my thoughts. So out of

Swedenborg's evidence from beyond earth's frontier I construct a world that shall measure up to the high claims of my spirit when I quit this wonderful but imprisoning house of clay.

Perhaps I may suggest another way of looking at Swedenborg's assertions that will be helpful. Science tells us of that strange, dark little chamber in the brain into which the sun and stars, the earth and ocean enter upon wings of light, and how from its mysterious abode the soul comes forth, and in twilight they commune together. Only He who made all things can gaze upon their unveiled glory. We could not behold their untempered splendour and live. That is why man is permitted to look at everything only as in a glass, darkly, and gaze only upon shadows in one small, dimly lighted chamber. Why should he speak of the "dim mysteries" of heaven so doubtingly when really he apprehends so little of earth and that only with veiled senses? Why cannot the soul with equal freedom go forth from its dwelling-place and, discarding the poor lenses of the body, peer through the telescopes of truth into the infinite reaches of immortality? At all events, this gives a key to Swedenborg's other-world records. He says it is the inner man who sees and perceives what goes on about him, and that from this interior source alone feeling and sensation have their life. But the illusion that all sense experience is outside of man is so common that the mind cannot get rid of it, except by practising concentration. I have not been especially bothered with this illusion because I am so constantly thrown upon my thoughts and imagination; but people prove it to me frequently when they express surprise that I can enjoy flowers and music and descriptions of lovely landscapes. If it is so unbelievably hard to make them understand the simplest facts about the potency of touch and smell, how are they going to form a valid judgment of another's position when he not only sees and hears bodily, but also uses his spiritual faculties to an exceptional degree, and thus widens the narrow ring which encircles things sensible into an almost limitless horizon?

## IV

THE Bible is the record of man's efforts to find God and learn how to live in harmony with his laws. Theologians have always endeavoured to grip in permanent form man's momentary impressions of God and the fleeting, changing aspects of his world. From this process have arisen many of the contradictions in the literal sense of the Bible, and misunderstandings of God's nature and His purpose. The Bible tells of man's halting beginning and gradual development, and the culminating perfection of the Christ-gospel. I conceive of this book as a spiritual "Iliad" covering many thousands of years, touching many nations—a splendid, variegated story, crossed at certain points by uninspired individual imaginings, dark periods of materialism, and illumined periods when the face of God shone upon the world, and there was light on field and sky and water, and in the minds of men. Out of the chaos of human experience an individual is now and then lifted to the peak of spiritual consciousness. As man develops, and his intelligence slowly unfolds, these individual peaks are more frequently seen; but they are never precisely alike. Each one is a light-bringer; but the light is so infinitely varied by the medium through which it is transmitted that it is sometimes difficult to perceive its Divine source.

Just as all things upon earth represent and image forth all the realities of another world, so the Bible is one mighty representative of the whole spiritual life of humanity. The characters come and pass before us. The lawgivers, the kings, the prophets—through the pages they pass. Like a mountain stream, the generations pass in endless procession, now praying, now weeping, now filling the cities with the voice of rejoicing, now walking in the evil imaginings of their hearts and making unto themselves graven images, now falling by the sword, mourning in captivity for the multitude of their transgressions, now bowing their heads to the will of Jehovah, now pouring imprecations upon their enemies, now building and marrying, now destroying, now singing songs of praise, now sacrificing, now comforting, now crucifying their Saviour.

In a book, the making of which has continued from generation to generation, inconsistencies and confusion are inevitable. Yet it is the most important record of the gropings of the human spirit that mankind possesses. Swedenborg set himself the task of separating the dross from the gold, the Word of God from the words of men. He had a genius for interpreting the sacred symbolism of the Bible similar to the genius of Joseph when he revealed the meaning of Pharaoh's dreams in the land of his captivity. The theologians of his time darkened counsel with many words without knowledge. While they were helpless before the curtains of the Shrine, Swedenborg drew them aside with subtle insight, and revealed the Holy of Holies in all its glory.

The Church had departed from the simple, direct, and inspiring story of how our Lord came upon earth clothed in visibility and dwelt as a man among men. For the marvellous reality, the clergy substituted fantasies that entangled them in metaphysical webs from which they could not extricate themselves. The beautiful truth of the Divine Humanity became distorted, dissociated, dissected beyond recognition, and our Lord Himself was lost in deadly dialectics. Swedenborg brought together the scattered and broken parts, gave them normal shape and meaning, and thus established a "new communion with God in Christ." Swedenborg was not a destroyer, but a divinely inspired interpreter. He was a prophet sent by God. His own message proclaims it more convincingly than any saying of his followers could. There is no escaping his virile personality. As we read his message, we are filled with recognition and delight. He did not make a new Bible, but he made the Bible all new! One who receives him gains a great spiritual possession.

The first and last thought of Swedenborg throughout his writings is to show that in the Bible, rightly read and interpreted, is to be found the truest and noblest conception of God possible. Most human minds are so constituted that there is in them a secret chamber where theological subjects are stored, and its centre is the idea of God. If this idea is false and cruel, all things which follow it by logical sequence partake of these qualities. For the highest is also the inmost, and it is the very essence of every belief and thought and institution derived from it. This essence, like a soul, forms everything it enters into an image of itself; and as it descends to the planes of daily life, it lays hold of the truths in the mind and infects them with its cruelty and error. Such was the idea of God in ancient India, where a highly intellectual class attempted to dictate the way of living on the principle that, to be like God, one must crush out all human affection and duties and relations; and the moment one became utterly passionless, without thought or interest in anything external, one was godlike—absorbed into the infinite, and ready for another world. This was an extreme case; but it illustrates the kind of beliefs that are hostile to humanity. By that I mean beliefs which set up fictitious excellences, encourage devotional feeling, and ceremonies which do not have for an object the good of mankind, and which are made substitutes for a righteous, useful life. Such beliefs darken all morality and make it an instrument of a supreme being worshipped indeed with adulation, but in truth repulsive to the good and the wise.

There is another spiritual danger against which Swedenborg often warns his readers—vagueness of thought about God. He says many times that humble folk think more wisely with all their blunders and superstitions about God, the soul and immortality, than many who have great knowledge, but who look into creation and into their own minds and find them empty of divine truth. How thrillingly significant the words of Jeremiah come back to uphold the groping believer: "Thus saith the Lord, let not the wise man glory in his wisdom; neither let the mighty man glory in his might; let not the rich man glory in his riches; but let him that glorieth glory in this, that he understandeth and knoweth me, that I am the Lord, who executeth loving-kindness, judgment, and right-eousness in the earth for in these things I delight, saith the Lord."

A wandering idea of an invisible God, Sweden-borg declares, "is not determined to anything; for this reason it ceases and perishes. The idea of God as a spirit, when a spirit is believed to be as ether or wind, is an empty idea; but the idea of God as Man is a just idea; for God is Divine Love and Divine Wisdom, with every quality belonging to them, and the subject of these is man, and not ether or wind."

Again we read: "If anyone thinks of the Divine itself without the idea of Divine Man, he thinks vaguely, and a vague idea is no idea at all; or he conceives an idea of the Divine from the visible universe without a boundary, or which ends in obscurity, which idea makes one with the idea of the worshippers of Nature; it also falls into Nature, and becomes no idea."

When the three-fold nature of the human being, spirit, intellect, and body, is rightly understood, it will be found that all forms he perceives pass into the imagination, and his soul endows them with life and meaning. Man and the universe are pictured in the Divine Mind. God created man in His own Image and Likeness, and in his turn man sends forth into his mind and body and the world thought-forms stamped with his whole individuality. It is known how the artist sees beautiful pictures in his mind before he paints them. Similarly, the spirit projects ideas into thought-images, or symbols; that is the universal and the only true language. If one could convey his joy or faith or his mental picture of a sunrise to another in visible form, how much more satisfactory that would be than the many words and phrases of ordinary language! I have cried when I touched an embossed Chinese symbol which represents happiness, and no amount of description would have produced such an effect upon me. It was a picture of a man with his mouth close to a rice field. How forcibly it brought home the fact that the Chinese are utterly dependent upon the rice they grow, and that when their fields are flooded, and the crops destroyed, starvation for millions of human beings is inevitable. Many ideas crowded into one symbol gain a power which words tend to neutralize. The French say that "words are employed to conceal ideas." Ruskin has an eloquent passage in "Sesame and Lilies," where he speaks of words as masks which draw the mind away from real issues to external things.

Now the Bible is largely written in this universal language. Of course Christians knew this before Swedenborg's day. They were familiar with the "dark sayings" and "parables"; but to them as to most of us a great many chapters, and the "Apocalypse" especially, were utterly unintelligible. "Verily, thou art a God that hidest thyself, O God of Israel, the Saviour," describes exactly the hidden truths of the Word. Israel did not know Him, except in the cloud and the pillar of fire and through the rod of His Power. When He caused Himself to be seen as Man upon earth, He was called an ally of the prince of devils! Even His own disciples mistook His purpose, and disputed among themselves as to who should be greatest in His Kingdom. They misinterpreted his Work of Love as a plan of conquest and personal glory. Over all His ways there is a covering! His very revelation is veiled in clouds. The Word which professes to show Him to us, clothes Him in the limitations of finite human nature, and we gain the most contradictory impressions of His attributes. He is infinite and eternal, and yet our human passions and ignorance are ascribed to Him. He says, "Fury is not in me," "I am not angry, you provoke yourselves unto anger," and yet He pours the fierceness of His wrath upon the earth. He is presented as a God who "doth not repent," and He does repent. He gives to each man according to his own works, and yet He visits the sins of the fathers upon the children. There is a long series of such apparent contradictions, and it is natural that many people cannot see any order underlying such a chaos of irreconcilable ideas. If we believe in a God at all worthy of love, we cannot think of Him as angry, capricious, or changeable. It seems as though these conceptions must have been part of the barbarism of the times when the Bible was written.

Swedenborg develops a philosophy of Divine revelation which is reasonable. He points out that, as in science, every revelation of new ideas from God must be suited to the states and the capacities of those who receive them. He undertakes to show that the literal statement of the Scriptures is an adaptation of Divine Truth to the minds of people who are very simple or sensuous or perverse. He demonstrates that there is a spiritual sense within the literal, suited to the higher intelligence of the angels who also read God's Truth and think with us, although they are invisible. In this superior sense is the fullness of Divine Truth. What would a friend care about what I said to him if he took my words literally? Would I not appear to him insane if he thought I meant to say that the sun rises and sets, or the earth is flat, or that I do not live in the dark? It is the meaning my friend listens to, not the words or the appearances which they convey.

That process is very similar to the one Swedenborg employs in finding out the deeper meaning of the Word. God appears small and undivine if a dull, perhaps bad man reads that He is angry with the wicked every day; but a man of sense and heart sees that it is only an appearance, and that we put off on Him our own anger with each other and the punishment we have brought upon ourselves. There is also the anger of the just which subsides in a moment, and is understood as love that chasteneth. But God is incapable even of sternness and He tells His people this over and over again. As we penetrate into His Divine Word, putting aside one covering after another, we find a Word truer and truer to His nature. He did not create man and then betray and reject him from Eden. He does not teach laws and break them and impute guilt to His creature. He warns, but does not cast anyone into hell or forsake him. It is man who constrains Him to express commandments in language that can be apprehended and acted upon. Swinburne was unconsciously feeling His Presence when he wrote these lines:

O my sons, too dutiful
Towards gods not of me,
Was I not enough beautiful?
Was it hard to be free?
For behold, I am with you, am in you and of you;
Look forth now and see.

Who ever realized the abuse that is piled up to
the heavens daily and hurled upon this more than
beautiful, all-enduring Deity! He does not really hide
Himself; but the determined evil speech of selfishness hides Him.

I have said all this because we need to have a
very clear, unclouded idea of God's nature if we are
to read the symbols of His Word connectedly. According to this theory, the spiritual sense deals with
the soul exclusively—its needs and trials, its changes
and renewals, not of times, places, and persons.
When we read of mountains, rivers, lambs and doves,
thunders and lightnings, golden cities and precious
stones and trees of life with healing leaves, we may
know they are exact symbols of the spiritual principles that lie back of them. Affections and ideas are
signified, and their uses to the soul are similar to
the uses of their natural representatives to the body.
This rule of interpretation was employed by Swedenborg for twenty-seven years, and he did not have to
change or correct one Scriptural statement given
in his first published work. He gives the same spiritual equivalent for the same natural object through-

As a child

With Anne Sullivan,
at age 38

At Radcliffe

Printed in U.S.A.

**With Polly Thomson**

**With Alexander Graham Bell**

**"Hearing" Jascha Heifetz**

**Helen Keller with the
Martha Graham dancers**

**Rabindranath Tagore met
Helen Keller in 1931**

**In conversation with her long-time friend, Mrs. Eleanor Roosevelt**

With her favorite
book—the Bible

In 1926 Helen Keller met
Calvin Coolidge. She was honored by every President since then

1961—Helen Keller meets President Kennedy

out the Bible, and the meanings fit wherever they are applied. I know, I have tried this key, and it fits. This is what Swedenborg calls the law of correspondences—analogies between the forms of nature and those of spirit. The Bible may be called the Poem of the World as well as God's finite utterance to man.

Swedenborg's works, especially the "Arcana Cœlestia," confirm much of what Ingersoll and other critics of the Bible say about the untrustworthiness of its literal statements; but at the same time it is demonstrated that they are quite wrong in their conclusions about its value from a different point of view. I have had abundant opportunity to learn how defective the sense of the letter is in the light of modern science, how strange some of the stories are, and how often they lack outward harmony. Nevertheless, I have also observed that there is a meaning beneath the letter that cannot be read in word but only in symbol, and this meaning holds good throughout the parts where it occurs. There is a compelling example of it in Psalm 78:

"I will open my mouth in a parable; I will utter dark sayings of old, which we have heard and known, and our fathers have told us." Then follows in the Psalm a summary of the experiences of the Israelites in Egypt, and their pilgrimage to Canaan. This record is true history; but here it is pronounced to be a parable which only the initiated can fully grasp.

And what a deep parable it is! It describes perfectly
our exodus from materialism and ignorance, and our
slow, difficult progress toward the happier life,
which the beautiful, fertile land of Canaan represents. I am giving this simply as an illustration of
how Swedenborg always regards the Bible as a ve-
hicle of Divine Truth.

It is of interest to recall that in the year 1753
Astruc made his famous discovery of two or more
documents in the Pentateuch and at that very time
Swedenborg was publishing, anonymously, in London, the "Arcana" explaining Genesis and Exodus.
The latter did not believe that Scripture had anything to do with the physical creation or a literal
deluge, or that the first eleven chapters of Genesis
were about individuals named Adam and Noah. It
was a very different phase of the subject which
came to his attention. He was enabled by the study
of Hebrew and by his mental illumination to see
that the early chapters gave an account in an ancient
parabolical style of the spiritual life of the race from
the beginning down to the Jewish era. He pointed
out that the first chapter contains the stages of
evolution by which the mind of man, at first dark
and chaotic, was developed until it reached the Eden
of simple truth and happiness. This age continued
until self-interest asserted its power, and the innocence of childhood was gradually lost. At last wrong
ideas flooded the world. Then a keen race of men,

denoted by Noah in the ark, began a new age. Intelligence grew rapidly, and the rod of conscience replaced the voice of the pure soul. The symbol was no longer a garden but a vineyard. Mankind grew up like an ambitious youth, building the great empires of the East whose records we are recovering year by year. The civilization of that period was extensive; but in time it declined. Polytheism and idolatry came into being. War and violence threatened to cover the face of the earth with ruins, and another dispensation had to be established. That was the beginning of the Jewish Church which kept monotheism alive until, in the fullness of time, Christianity dawned upon the world. The first Christian Church, or civilization, was essentially a continuation of the Mosaic one—full of the rough makeshifts and tallow candles and flickering torches of a faith fitted to a turbulent society. The sense-pictures and fair engravings of ritual and the sceptre of authority beheld, as it were, in the margin of the Word were superstitiously revered; but the Divine Meaning remained unread. So passed the perverse manhood of the world, and we continue to feel its passionate outbreaks and downfalls and unhappy moods. But now the arc light of a more enlightened faith shines upon humanity, and the creation of a new man goes on step by step; yea, the Sabbath of peace in all hearts and in the outer world shall yet come, and the reign of selfish, blind instincts shall vanish forever. Thus

the Bible is portrayed as one vast glorious parable.
All the way one may read in it lessons of life and
its phases—its first innocence, its youthful wayward-
ness, its saving conversion, and its incalculable possibilities of service and joy. It is a complete circle
from paradise to paradise—"the circle of the earth
upon which sitteth the Lord forever." The limited
language and imperfect modes of thought of days
long gone by are only the body of a heavenly message that declares God to be always with us, imparting new and higher gifts and capabilities.

The higher criticism of the Bible, as Swedenborg
indicates, does not take away a jot or tittle of its
essential meaning, but corrects erroneous views of
the early Jewish writers.

In this view, then, there is no conflict with the
accumulating data of archæology, geology, and
the study of different documents. The Bible is lifted
to a higher level than ever before, and is clothed
with holiness. The old view was most unworthy of
the Great God of all souls. He was supposed to have
said nothing until Sinai. He had left no room for
science to work without making trouble for faith.
His instruction of the race had been through the
narrow and exclusive ray of light to Moses. His
providences were chiefly heartless neglects. All nations except Israel were under His ban, and millions
must have been swept into the abyss. Then His
"beloved Son" interceded, and offered himself up as

sacrifice upon the Cross for an otherwise doomed race, then the "Father" was propitiated, and cancelled His sentence, but only for persons in whose behalf the "Son" spoke a good word! This old view was Swedenborg's arch enemy; for it was constantly taught in the schools, preached and proclaimed with the utmost zeal and eloquence. Its gigantic shadow lay on the baby's cradle, brooded over the prison and the death-bed, it has penetrated even the smallest acts and common sayings of every day. Skeptics and atheists naturally sprang up everywhere. Faith in the Lord and His Word seemed to demand the suppression of science and philosophy and the smothering of all generous sentiments.

But Swedenborg confronted this giant with a new view that brought fresh hope and appreciation of the Bible. The God he followed is the God of all nations and all times. Infinitely patient and unselfish, He has watched over the whole world. At first He led childlike man by the same law of spontaneous growth by which He forms a beautiful tree; then He taught him in the parables of garden, flood, vineyard, and tower, afterward in the books of Moses and the Prophets. As to geology and other sciences, pictures from them are used to symbolize the regeneration of man. There always have been laws of justice in every land; and the code of Hammurabi, who was Amraphel in Genesis, is well known. But the Decalogue was given at Sinai in a peculiar manner, so that it might prefigure the spiritual laws which wisdom and science were to reveal as the centuries passed. Only by having definite pictures of life stamped upon our memories can we learn to imagine more beautiful ones and make them living realities. Whenever the Jews turned aside from their trust for all men, they were rebuked pointedly with the example of many other peoples who did not have the Word in writing, but upon whose wise and noble minds the truth was inscribed as with letters of gold. Swedenborg holds up many of the Gentiles of his day as examples of sincerity and well-doing which should put Christendom to shame, and lo! now it is they who are showing the most determined courage for the cause of brotherhood, while we devise more effective ways to kill one another in the next war. Truly, the Word of the Lord stands forever, though the old heaven and earth of literalism melt away.

If it is indicated in Swedenborg's teachings that evolution is the Divine method of creating, he also shows that it is not complete without previous "involution." Since God is Life itself or Soul, He cannot help putting a form of soul into everything that comes from His Hand, and each soul takes hold of matter and shapes it into the image of something which God has thought. It is still true, as Plato taught, that something cannot be made out of nothing, and intelligence cannot be evolved out of matter because it lies in such a different plane of existence. Although man has been developed from a lower to a higher form, yet he has been immortal from the beginning. He did not, however, enjoy his higher capacities until he became conscious of the soul within him. It is also asserted that he has fallen from a childlike simplicity and innocence, while he has made tremendous material progress, and is returning by long, steep ways to the heights where is God, "the meeting place of all souls."

Swedenborg's revelations take from every grave its fear. Before he was raised up into heaven, the future life was, for most "Christians," full of terrors. It was a disputed question whether life or death brought greater opportunity—whether death was the end of life or the door to another existence. Now we are positive that the larger, nobler life is beyond the grave. The child dying in his mother's arms was an intolerable thought. Now we know of the sweet, unclouded childhood which awaits him, the bright abodes where angels will teach him to speak, think creative thoughts and do the work for which he is best fitted, where he will grow up in beauty and go forth to deeds and adventures mightier than were ever beheld upon earth. We know now that every faithful love which has been thwarted here has tenfold greater joy in store for it on the other side. Heaven and hell have become facts in our deeper consciousness about which there can be no dispute. We have an intuitive certainty of them—

not a halting knowledge inferred from arguments or reasons which we can accept or reject as we choose. Only such face-to-face knowledge gives reality to things, since it springs from life, and Swedenborg's living testimony will shed a low but ever-increasing light upon the dark "hinterland" of our soul experience, and reinforce our groping efforts with the daring of immortal purpose.

It is all very well to talk about the folly of other-worldliness, but men have tried living without it and ended in tragic failure. It is true, only a very few of us see the way out; but these words were dictated to Swedenborg: "Truths derived from good have all power." If we only let the Lord inspire us from His Divine Truth, the strength of Samson shall pass into us mentally, and we shall yet be able to lift the dead weight that shuts the vast majority of the race out from their splendid possibilities of development. It is significant that Emerson, who stood at a great distance from Swedenborg in many beliefs, saw the fundamental truth of his selfless attitude, and wrote: "The weakness of the will begins when the individual would be something of himself. And the blindness of the intellect begins when it would be something of itself." Nothing but letting the Divine Life have its way through us will deliver the world.

This is the true significance of Swedenborg's message from "the hills whence cometh our help."

It was not immortality he stressed, but the responsibilities it imposes upon us. He did not regard his extraordinary intercourse with angels as an end itself, but as a means of opening his understanding to a true interpretation of God's Word, and of making the knowledge thus acquired the common heritage of mankind.

So it must be understood that, while the possibility of communicating with departed spirits is conceded, we are never encouraged to cultivate it. When prophets, apostles, and seers are needed to wake the sleeping hearts of men, it is useful for them to be in conscious association with angels and devils because the Lord then supervises the work Himself, and prevents confusion. But as a rule, such intercourse exposes man to great danger, because he is so easily influenced by deceiving spirits who know his weaknesses, and use him for selfish purposes.

If, therefore, Swedenborg states that every human being is attended by at least two angels from heaven, and two bad spirits from hell, he also maintains that our peace of mind and orderliness of life depend upon our being unconscious of our invisible allies and enemies. As John Wesley rightly said, we have all we need to know in those revelations, and the rest is for us to follow the Lord alone, trusting to His protection and guidance.

The Lord Jesus Christ is named in the begin-

ning and in the closing sentence of the Book of
Revelation; He is the central figure of the book.
He is the Jesus of the New Testament. "Revelation" is the sequel to the Gospels, which tell of the
Lord's work upon earth, His crucifixion and His
resurrection. The Apocalypse tells how He has continued His work in the might of His glorified Humanity—the supreme Example and Inspirer. In the
Gospels He said, "Lo, I am with you alway, even
unto the end of the world"; and He often spoke of
the comfort and enlightenment He would yet bring
to men.

What has become of this promise? Except for
the coming of the Holy Spirit on the Day of Pente-
cost, the wisdom to teach and the courage and joy
which the disciples felt for a short time, the Promise
appears to have been quite forgotten.

But Swedenborg shows that "Revelation" takes
up this Promise and prophesies its fulfilment. By
symbols it pictures the nature of the risen Lord, the
blessings which flow from His Presence, and tells
explicitly what we must do to prepare our minds
for Him. It gives fully the ideals of Christian life
which shine like stars around this glorious Presence,
and which are only faintly outlined by the Apostles;
it exposes the cruel beliefs and evils of life which
must be overcome before these ideals can become a part of ourselves. It shows the chief obstacles
to true Christianity—faith without charity, and the

greed for domination by means of rituals and superstitions and terror. The beasts arising out of the
sea and the bottomless pit represent such mental
monsters as predestination, intellectual bondage, and
the idea of three gods, which has divided men's
minds and rendered "one-pointed" conduct impossible, as the Hindoos would say. For such ideas
destroy all power of spiritual concentration, breed
unbalanced emotions, tear asunder the texture of
ethics, and drive away philosophy which lives only
in the Unity of God. The dragon of "Revelation"
is every effort of unscrupulous men to reason away
the Divinity of the Lord, and the necessity of keeping His commandments. Babylon is all pride and
conceit that prevent the acknowledgment of Him
and a life according to His Truth.

Many chapters of the Apocalypse are full of
scenes of judgment in the world of spirits. Seals
are opened, and trumpets sound, which means that
the darkness and hypocrisy of a decadent church
are uncovered. Through all the scenes moves the
Lord in His Divine Humanity. The strength of His
Love, the purity of His Wisdom and the zeal of
His Providence are symbolized by the golden girdle
about His breast, His head like snow, and His eyes
like flames of fire and His face shining as the
sun in all its glory. His voice like many waters is
the spreading of new thoughts and higher beliefs
into the systems of earth. He clearly tells herein

why His Presence has been so little felt since the days when He walked upon the earth, beheld by mortal eyes, and why there has been such small comfort from His Spirit. Dominion and oppression have robbed Him of us, as it were, and the Church in past ages has so narrowed education that man's thought has been long coming up to the degree of knowledge necessary for a new message from Him.

From the scenes of Judgment He turns to gladden heaven and earth with His smile as the New Jerusalem descends—a new dispensation. We read, "The tabernacle of God is with men," and again, "I saw no temple therein; for the Lord God Almighty and the Lamb are the temple of it." The Lord's own human nature is the "tabernacle of God with men," the Temple of His Presence.

Swedenborg interprets the measure of the Holy City—a full, generous measure, the measure of that perfect manhood attained by the Lord in the world. The waters flowing from the throne of God are abundant, refreshing truths from His Word for those who truly unite their lives with His. For the acknowledgment of the Divine Humanity of the Lord is the wisdom which opens the inexhaustible fountains of truth in Old Testament parables, psalms and prophecies, in the Gospels, and especially in this long-sealed book of "Revelation."

How divinely beautiful it all is when rightly understood! The picture of the seven candlesticks and in the midst of them one like unto the Son of Man stands as the frontispiece of this book, and, under the inspired touch of Swedenborg's mind, it grows brighter and richer until it culminates in the vision of the City with the river of life and the tree with leaves of healing for all nations, and the sunshine of the Lord's own Presence, never again to be hidden from His children.

Swedenborg's two books explaining the Apocalypse are a fulfilment of the age-long prophecy in the mind of him who sees "the Son of Man coming in the clouds of heaven with power and great glory." For to "see" is to understand, "the clouds of heaven" are the letter of the Word, and "the Son of Man coming" is the Lord in the power and glory of the Spiritual Sense shining through the Letter. Above the Cross was placed the inscription, "Jesus of Nazareth, King of the Jews," written in Hebrew, Greek, and Latin, foreshadowing as it were the time when the Lord would satisfy longing souls with His likeness, revealing the hidden meanings of the Hebrew Word, and the Greek New Testament in Greek, and giving the Spiritual Sense in Latin. In this language Swedenborg wrote, translating, as the Lord taught him, the symbols of the Bible into principles of practical life for the use and happiness of mankind. He did not even put his name to many of his works. "Servant of the Lord Jesus Christ" was his pen name. He said, "It is not unknown to

me that many will say that a man can never speak
with spirits and angels while he lives in the body;
and many that it is fantasy, others that I state such
things to gain credit, others other things; but I do
not hesitate on this account, for I have seen, have
heard, have touched."

I have read with wonderment that students of
psychic life like Sir Oliver Lodge have scarcely referred to Swedenborg's voluminous works dealing
with the same subject. Sir Oliver Lodge has published a number of interviews with his "dead" son,
Raymond, who told how the inhabitants of eternity
do the work they like best and live in the company
they like best, how they are fed and clothed. But
the information thus conveyed is scanty and fragmentary. It was extracted by elaborate rappings,
and in a manner not at all resembling Swedenborg's face-to-face conversations with angels and
spirits, or his superhuman poise while he noted
down a multitude of rational happenings and visible
truths sparkling like diamonds. He saw memory ossi-
fied, he heard the complaints of bad spirits when
they looked into heaven and saw thick darkness.
He found that angels could not breathe in an atmosphere to which their thoughts had not raised them
and he saw the delicious fruits of charity which
nourish both body and mind!

When we think of all those who would rejoice
to have colourful details of that Unseen World to

which their loved ones have gone, the sacred responsibility of satisfying their doubting hearts is obvious. They can rejoice to know that one hundred and seventy-five years ago there arose a trained scientist who, contrary to all his expectations and plans, and the wishes of his mother, found himself a seer, and gave to the world without any profit for himself twenty-seven stout octavo volumes crammed full of details of definite contacts with the spiritual universe! He stood right up to his claim, let his wealth go, lived simply, printed all his own works, distributed them in a humble yet dignified manner. He remained cool in temperament, weighing all he did and said. He never showed signs of being racked by passion or impulse or any excitement of a supernatural kind. He never forsook his inductive habits of thinking or denied any sensuous truths or scorned the smallest joys of his fellow men. No matter how absorbed he might be in his staggering mission, he responded to every demand for his assistance or sympathy in the practical needs of daily life. On his death-bed he was asked if all he had written was strictly true, or if he wished any parts to be excepted, and he replied with unfaltering warmth: "I have written nothing but the truth, as you will have it more confirmed hereafter all the days of your life, provided you always keep close to the Lord, and faithfully serve Him alone, in shunning evils of all kinds as sins against Him, and diligently search His Word, which from beginning to end bears incontestable testimony to the truth of the doctrines I have delivered to the world."

## V

GUIDED by the light of the Divine Word, Swedenborg saw the Oneness of God in Essence and Person, and Jesus Christ as God in the humanity which he assumed on earth, and the Holy Spirit the Infinite Power for creating and maintaining goodness and happiness. This Truth is the centre of all sound Christian teaching, and unless one perceives it clearly, the Scriptures cannot be rationally explained. So one can joyously cherish the One God without denying but rather infinitely exalting Jesus Christ—that beautiful Personality toward whom millions of hearts have yearned during the ages.

> For all must love the human form,
>     In heathen, Turk, or Jew:
> Where mercy, love, and pity dwell
>     There God is dwelling too.

The joy inspired by such a concept of the Lord is like the sun with its three-fold glory of warmth, light, and activity. It is like the satisfaction with which one beholds the happy balance of soul, mind, and body in a beautiful human being, or the perfect sequence of seed sprouting into blossom, and the

blossom yielding luscious fruit. How sane and easy
and capable of fitting into the nature of all things
such a concept is! Yet what prodigious effort it cost
Swedenborg to plant it so that it could grow and
flourish! He uprooted vast encumbrances of argu-
ment and conjecture on the Trinity and justifica-
tion by faith alone, just as Francis Bacon substituted direct observation of Nature for the scholastic
method of deductive reasoning. They both obeyed
the call of everlasting Truth, committed themselves
to the difficulties and the solitude of a new era,
and upheld their opinions against the hostility of
public opinion with the hope that they might provide
for coming generations a guidance more faithful and
secure. They both found that "the doctrines which
find most favour with the populace are either con-
tentious and pugnacious, or specious and empty,
so that no doubt the greatest wits have been very
fain for reputation's sake to bow to the judgment
of the time and the multitude."

Swedenborg could also have said with Bacon,
"This degenerate kind of learning did reign chiefly
amongst the schoolmen, who, having sharp and
strong wits and abundance of leisure, did, out of
no great quantity of matter, and infinite agitation
of wit, spin unto us those laborious webs of learning which are extant in their books."

The new thoughts about the Unity of God which
Swedenborg offered to replace the old are pre-

cious because they give one the insight to distinguish between the real Deity and the repelling appearance with which a wrong reading of the Word and the anthropomorphic attributes with which passion-driven men have invested Him. The following extracts from his "True Christian Religion" show how he strove to supplant those unchristian concepts with a nobler faith:

"God is omnipotent, because He has all power from Himself, and all others have power from Him. His power and His will are one, and because He wills nothing but what is good, therefore He can do nothing but what is good. In the spiritual world, no one can do anything contrary to his will; this they derive there from God whose power and will are one. God also is good itself; therefore, while He does good, He is in Himself and cannot go out of Himself. From this it is manifest that His omnipotence proceeds and operates within the sphere of the extension of good, which is infinite.

"It may be evident how delirious they are who think, still more they who believe, and yet more they who teach, that God can condemn anyone, curse anyone, cast anyone into hell, predestine the soul of anyone to eternal death, avenge injuries, be angry or punish. He cannot even turn away His face from man and look at him with a hard countenance."

"It is a prevailing opinion at this day, that the

omnipotence of God is like the absolute power of
a king in the world who can at his pleasure do whatever he wills, absolve and condemn whom he pleases,
make the guilty innocent, declare the faithless faithful, exalt the unworthy and undeserving above the
worthy and deserving; nay, that he can under whatever pretext deprive his subjects of their goods,
and sentence them to death; with other such things.
From this absurd opinion, faith, and doctrine con-
cerning the Divine omnipotence, as many falsities,
fallacies, and chimeras have flowed into the church
as there are subjects, divisions, and derivations of
faith therein; and as many more may yet flow in
as pitchers might be filled with water from a large
lake, or as serpents that creep out of their holes
and bask in the sunshine in the desert of Arabia.
What need is there of more than two words, omnipotence and faith; and then to spread before the people conjectures, fables, and trifles, as many as occur
to the senses of the body? For reason is banished
from them both; and when reason is banished, in
what does the thought of man excel the reason of a
bird that flies over his head?"

Such teachings lift one up to a mountain sum-
mit where the atmosphere is clear of hatred, and
one can perceive that the nature of the Divine
Being is Love and Wisdom and Use, and that He
never changes in His attitude toward anyone at
any time. It is shown that all men cannot be made

better because some are incapable of desiring self-improvement. Some people never find God. Those who think constantly of themselves never see visions. Their souls drown in the materiality that rises about them like a flood and sweeps them beyond their level. They see nothing but others who are struggling in the dark waters like themselves. They are indifferent to saving themselves or helping anyone else. But all through Swedenborg's books shines an image of the Eternal Love which embraces every human being, and seeks to restrain him from sinking into deeper sin. It is explained why the Lord is called "deaf and blind" in Isaiah—that He is as though He does not see the sins of men; for He does not chastise or break His children, but gently bends and turns them to good as far as they will yield to His influence and coöperate with Him.

Another doctrine, revolutionary in those days, is that there is no such thing as predestination to hell, that all are born for heaven, as the seed is born to become a flower and the little thrush in the nest is intended to become a song-bird, if the laws of life are obeyed. In other words, all have been redeemed, and all can be regenerated, and it is a man's own fault if he lives and thinks himself out of heaven. But he does go there every time he thinks a noble thought; and he stays when it has become his happiness to serve others.

Some have said that Darwin made a laughing-stock

of heaven and hell; but they are made no laughing-
stock in Swedenborg's writings, and they never
should be from anyone else's point of view, so
long as men are capable of sinning and feeling re-
morse. We are taught there is no hell of the medi-
æval kind; but there is a mental hell into which people go who are self-confirmed lovers of evil, and
who wilfully deny God in their heart. They do not
fall into literal fire, and as they punish themselves
more than enough, God takes away from them even
the anguish of conscience. That is why they are
never forced to put themselves into states of heavenly feeling—they would only be suffocated and
robbed of the only pleasures they have. But they
"burn" with selfish instincts and love of dominion.
They see as they think—like owls and bats. They
debate and litigate and fight; they practise endless
arts of magic and "faking," they must labour hard
for air and food, and some of them seem always
to be cutting wood and mowing grass because on
earth they worked so furiously for rewards. Misers
hug to their hearts imaginary money-bags. Sirens
try painfully to beautify their pitiful forms and enjoy their images reflected in the dull light as of a
charcoal fire. Each gang of crooks strives to out-
wit all the rest, and the fierce joy of rivalry shines
luridly on their marred faces. Those who have
held tenaciously to their cruel, stupid opinions
talk hour after hour to their own idiotic kind and

to dumb spirits. When they are weary of their
futile efforts, all the genii, gnomes, enchanters, and
robbers take hands and dance, like the crazy fantasies of a fevered dream.

But these unfortunate beings are not left useless
or despised by the Lord. He brings them into external order, and, as far as they can be led by
their affections, He induces them for the sake of
self to be of service to others. They enable man to
see the evil he is to avoid as well as the good he is
to choose. They keep alive the fires of ambition in
him when he does not care about ideals or the
public welfare, but desires rather fame and honour.
They sharpen some minds for unpleasant truths
which the children of light must surely learn if they
are to help guard humanity against brute force and
every form of oppression whether it be by one or
by many. Even the worst of the devils never escape
the sense of attraction they feel toward Him they
would fain deny, especially as He alone has the divine grace of always being near them, and tender
with their follies. Let anyone who would rage
against his fellow men as fools and evildoers be-
ware, even though they may clearly prove everything they say to be just. Truly, as Balzac asserted,
"Swedenborg has absolved God from the reproach
attached to Him in the estimation of tender souls,
for the perpetuity of revenge to punish the sin of
the moment—a system of injustice and cruelty."

According to all Swedenborg's testimony, after death we are like travellers going from place to place, making the acquaintance of all kinds of interesting objects, meeting all sorts of people and receiving something from each individual on the way. We observe, judge, criticize, and listen to words of wisdom or folly. We drop an opinion, take up another, sift it and test it in our mental crucible. From each new experience we extract finer kinds of knowledge and those truer intellectual concepts which are the property of all. On earth man lives apart, though not alone, and the most wonderful thoughts that he has known, through lack of listeners, have never been said. But in the other life it is different. All live together and learn together. All spirit beings, good and bad, are minds, and they communicate to each other instantly volumes of ideas which would require long periods to apprehend upon earth! So we shall journey onward, choosing the comrades best suited to us, and grow increasingly interested, wiser, saner, nobler, and happier through all eternity. What a prospect this opens up to those whose spirit wings are fretted by the uninspired facts of mortality! What an inexpressible comfort to those who hunger for lofty friendship and living intercourse! I believe that in heaven friendships may endure, as indeed they do on earth, by changing as well as by their steadfastness. For it is their nature to vitalize and diver-

sify the ideas and emotions which enter the field
of consciousness. Here below we are inclined to
lay stress on likeness and ignore difference; but in
heaven, and sometimes here among us, too, friends
similar in spirit are so different they offset or com-
plement each other like varied and beautiful colours
in the sunrise. They discover each other, and give
and receive the best that is in them. They do for
each other's souls what our acquaintances do when
they feed and clothe our bodies. A feeling of amaze-
ment comes over me as I realize how fully I know
this from experience. I am the happy object of
a rare friendship which makes my teacher a seer
of the capabilities folded away in me that darkness and silence would hide from most people.
There are moments in our lives so lovely, they
transcend earth, and anticipate heaven for us. This
foretaste of eternity has made clear to me the perpetual and all-embracing service that friendship
should ever be.

The Bible says that in heaven we "rest from our
labours"; but that only means when we have
worked out our salvation through sorrow, failure,
and temptation, we reach the Sabbath of peace and
innocence. The "labours" we rest from are the
obstacles of the flesh, the struggle for bread, cloth-
ing and shelter, war, and sordid schemes to outdo
each other for gain or power. But immense fields
of glorious work and emulation and endless interest

await all of us who are faithful over a few tasks
here. The employments in the Kingdom of Uses,
as heaven is called, cannot here be enumerated or
described specifically; for they are infinitely varied.
Those with unselfish parental love adopt and take
care of little ones from earth. Some educate boys
and girls, others give instruction to the simple and
earnest who desire it. Again, all the gentile nations
are taught new truths to enlarge and refine their
limited beliefs. There are special societies to attend
everyone who rises through death into Life, to de-
fend such newcomers into the arena of the middle
world against the unfriendliness of evil spirits, to
keep guard over those who inhabit the hell and
prevent them from tormenting each other beyond
endurance, and thus to lessen their sense of misery
as far as may be possible. Since all human beings
live both in this natural world and in the spiritual
realm at the same time, angels from every society
are chosen to guard men, take away little by little
their lusts and wrong habits of thought, and tenderly turn their love of dark deeds into the joy of
deeds of light. Only unwillingness in a man ever re-
strains their loving ministries and, even then, they
keep returning with steadfast faith and patience, for
they are, are they not, images and messengers of
the Divine Fidelity? They scarcely see and still less
dwell upon anyone's faults, but instead they study all
his beauties of disposition and mind, and interpret

the opposites into good. By following their genius closely, men and women who are becoming angels rise continually to nobler tasks, and each new state brings them an influx of new powers, which is meant by the Lord's promise of "full measure, shaken down, pressed together, and running over." The golden harps and the singing of endless praises, which have called forth so much adverse comment, and given such an unfavourable impression of lazy saints, are only pictorial appearances—the heart playing softly on its lyre of joy and singing as the task grows ever more beautiful and satisfying.

So, in the light of Swedenborg's teachings, heavenly life is a truly human life, and there are all kinds of service, domestic, civil, social, and inspirational, to be performed and enjoyed.

We are also informed that there are three kinds of angels—those whose chief interest is knowledge and the practical work that protects the outposts of heaven against intrusions of hell, those who philosophize and originate new ideas, and, finally, those who do not need to reason things out because they can feel with another, put themselves in his place by powers of perception and act directly and quickly. The character of these last might be compared with the fig tree, which does not stop to blossom, but brings forth its leaves and fruit at the same time. No one is quite like another, and thus there are innumerable groupings or societies;

but there is only one heaven—or heaven is one, just as the human body is one, though composed of countless organs, members, blood-vessels, nerves, and fibres. All lesser ends are subordinated to the common good. In a word, every glory, every ideal, every high desire—all that the dreams of noblest minds have ever whispered, and infinitely more un-thought-of possibilities, become substantial realities in the eternal sunshine of immortality.

In heaven, too, we shall find the beauty of woman and the strength of man, self-less love between the sexes, the frolic of children, the joys of companion-ship, and the vital power of touch exquisitely sooth-ing and eloquent.

If it is true that Swedenborg brings a clear, authoritative revelation of heavenly life as it can be best understood—free from all material limita-tions, we should have a definite idea of the purpose of education there. Now, that heavenly world is a vast realm of souls clothed with spiritual bodies, all interrelated and bound together in one magnifi-cent system of uses. There is not a single individual in all that multitude who has not capabilities, inter-ests, and knowledge of a special kind that make possible his own higher development and thereby the greater good of all. While they depend one upon another, each being grows more perfect in his own way, and becomes more responsive to the happiness which is increasingly bestowed upon him.

If we examine the life of earth intelligently, we shall find it also governed by the same Law of Use. Science teaches us that the body exists each part for the benefit of every other part. God breathes a similar purpose into Nature. The mineral kingdom is united, and serves as a support for the vegetable. The vegetable gives life to man, and both minister to humanity. This law of benefit from each to all and all to each is meant to rule in human life. Many have perverted it, and live on the labour and the brains of others; but sooner or later retribution overtakes them, and they must lay their offering of service on the altar of the common good, or drop out of the ranks of worthy humanity. This service may be rendered in any of three ways, with the hand, the intellect, and our emotional and æsthetic capacities.

Of course, if we view man subjectively, the case may be different. A person may mar his use by selfishness; but the fact remains that, objectively, our whole life and its environment teach the Law of Use, and are the best possible means for us to realize our proper ideals. It is for us to learn how to use that Law as our guide. We should seek ways to render it possible for each one to select the special activity that shall bring him interest and satisfaction and also harmonize with the good of all the rest. Then each one would find his place in the eternal Life of Use; this is the only right method of living in this or any other world.

The type of education we need, and the one which thoughtful people now urge, is that which will help us to appreciate this Law of Use, adapt it to ourselves, and choose the work in which we can best fulfil it. We need a system of education which may teach us about all the varieties of use that surround us and show the difference between the practical, the mental, and the spiritual services we can render, and which may impel each one to choose the task to which his interest and fitness draw him most strongly.

The reason why Swedenborg keeps holding up the heaven life as a pattern is that it serves as an object-lesson. The old thought tells us we are given earth to prepare for heaven, but there is truth in the other way round. We are given a knowledge of heaven to fit us better for earth. The Vision of Beauty must come into the workshop of Nazareth. So I do not hesitate to point to what Swedenborg says about the education of children in heaven as a suggestion for our earthly schools. There they are taught largely by "representations"—that is, by pictures, instructive plays, and scenes which they visit, that is by illustration and example. They are led to choose the uses they like best and are educated for them. This seems to be the goal toward which modern pedagogy is advancing. Incidentally,

I remember happily how I was led to the blessings of knowledge and accomplishment by a similar method, and I am confident that with wise modifications it can be of great use in our general educational system.

I can easily believe that, as Swedenborg often tries to show us, the visible and tangible phenomena of the other world are the direct embodiments of the mental states of its inhabitants. It is of little use to know about even the most wonderful splendours of heaven unless we understand somewhat of their origin and their essential meaning, and naturally this is difficult for others who do not sense the separateness between their earthly bodies and their inner selves. It is the combination of familiar objects in an immediate way with unfamiliar subjects that makes it all so strange. It is like learning a new language, and many of the fundamental facts which the language expresses.

What is so sweet as to awake from a troubled dream and behold a beloved face smiling upon you? I love to believe that such shall be our awakening from earth to heaven. My faith never wavers that each dear friend I have "lost" is a new link between this world and the happier land beyond the morn. My soul is for the moment bowed down with grief when I cease to feel the touch of their hands or hear a tender word from them; but the light of faith never fades from my sky, and I take heart

again, glad that they are free. I cannot understand
why anyone should fear death. Life here is more
cruel than death—life divides and estranges, while
death, which at heart is life eternal, reunites and
reconciles. I believe that when the eyes within my
physical eyes shall open upon the world to come, I
shall simply be consciously living in the country of
my heart. My steadfast thought rises above the trea-
son of my eyes to follow sight beyond all temporal
seeing! Suppose there are a million chances against
that one that my loved ones who have gone are
alive. What of it? I will take that one chance and
risk mistake, rather than let my doubts sadden their
souls, and find out afterward. Since there is that
one chance of immortality, I will endeavour not to
cast a shadow upon the joy of the departed. I sometimes wonder who needs cheer most, the one that
gropes on here below or the one that is perhaps
just learning truly to see in God's light. How real is
the darkness to one who only guesses in the shadows of earth at an unseen sun! But how well
worth the effort it is to keep spiritually in touch
with those who have loved us to their last moment
upon earth! Certainly, it is one of our sweetest experiences that when we are touched by some noble
affection or pure joy, we remember the dead most
tenderly, and feel powerfully drawn to them. And
always the consciousness of such a faith has the
power to change the face of mortality, make adver-

sity a winning fight, and set up a beacon of encouragement for those whose last support of joy seems taken from them. There is no such thing as "other worldliness" when we are convinced that heaven is not beyond us, but within us. We are only urged so much the more to act, to love, to hope against hope and resolutely to tinge the darkness about us with the beautiful hues of our indwelling heaven, Here and Now.

I read with emotion the words of Sir Humphrey Davy, in whom science and faith and unselfishness were combined to a remarkable degree: "I envy no quality of mind or intellect in others—not genius, power, wit, or fancy; but if I could choose what would be most delightful, and I believe most useful to me, I should prefer a firm religious belief to any other blessing; for it makes life a discipline of goodness, creates new hopes when all earthly hopes vanish; and throws over the decay, the destruction of existence, the most gorgeous of all lights; awakens life even in death, and from corruption and decay calls up beauty and divinity; makes an instrument of torture and shame the ladder of ascent to Paradise; and far above all combinations of earthly hopes, calls up the most delightful visions of palms and amaranths, the gardens of the blest, the security of everlasting joys, where the sensualist and the skeptic view only gloom, decay, annihilation, and despair." It is like a Pentecostal experience thus to feel in my hand the strong hand of a calm scientific man and a lover of mankind, who had no reconciler to second his thought, who saw the countless contradictions of the old faiths, who toiled in poverty at the first and then gave his invention of the safety-lamp to the world free, who knew the tortures of natural existence, but who kept unshaken his communion with his God.

Truly I have looked into the very heart of darkness, and refused to yield to its paralyzing influence, but in spirit I am one of those who walk the morning. What if all dark, discouraging moods of the human mind come across my way as thick as the dry leaves of autumn? Other feet have travelled that road before me, and I know the desert leads to God as surely as the green, refreshing fields and fruitful orchards. I, too, have been profoundly humiliated, and brought to realize my littleness amid the immensity of creation. The more I learn, the less I think I know, and the more I understand of my sense-experience, the more I perceive its shortcomings and its inadequacy as a basis of life. Sometimes the points of view of the optimist and the pessimist are placed before me so skilfully balanced that only by sheer force of spirit can I keep my hold upon a practical, liveable philosophy of life. But I use my will, choose life and reject its opposite, nothingness. Edwin Markham has exquisitely wrought into his poem "Take Your Choice," the opposing moods and different beliefs which contend for supremacy to-day:

On the bough of the rose-tree is the prickling briar:
The delicate lily must live in the mire;
The hues of the butterfly go at a breath;
At the end of the road is the house of death.

Nay, nay! On the briar is the delicate rose;
In the mire of the river the lily blows;
The moth is as fair as the flower of the sod;
At the end of the road is a door to God!

## VI

RELIGION has been defined as the science of our relations to God and to our fellow men and what we owe to ourselves. Surely Christianity, rightly understood, is the Science of Love. When the Lord dwelt upon earth visible to mortals, He declared that on the two commandments, Love of God and Love of the Neighbour, "hang all the Law and the Prophets." Who could know the Scriptures, and all human thought for that matter, as profoundly as did the gentle Nazarene charged with His divine mission? He emphasized the divine necessity of love all through the Gospels. "God is Love, God is Love, God is Love!" was the invariable meaning of such phrases as these, "If ye love me, keep my commandments"; "This is Life eternal, that they might know thee, the only true God, and Jesus Christ, whom thou hast sent"; "Seek ye first the Kingdom of God and his righteousness, and all these things [happiness and material blessings] shall be added unto you"; "I am the Way, the Truth, and the Life." He always visualized hatred as the opposite of God in every detail, great or small, and His teaching about hell was not as of punishment by God, but the inevitable law of evil recoiling upon those who cast themselves into hate and the burning lust and the

114

cruel miseries of wounded pride and thwarted ego-
ism. No matter from what angle He started, He came
back to this fact, that He entrusted the reconstruc-
tion of the world, not to wealth or caste or power or
learning, but to the better instincts of the race—to
the nobler ideals and sentiments of the people—to
love, which is the mover of the will and the dynamic
force of action. He turned His words every conceivable way and did every possible work to convince the doubters that love—good or evil—is the
life of their life, the fuel of their thoughts, the breath
of their nostrils, their heaven or their destruction.
There was no exception or modification whatever
in His holy, awful, supreme Gospel of love.

Yet for two thousand years, so-called believers
have repeated "God is Love" without sensing the
universe of truth contained in these three momentous
words or feeling their stimulating power. As a matter
of fact, ever since men began seriously to philosophize about life, there has been a sinister silence on
this noblest of all subjects. In the history of love as a
doctrine is a revelation of the tragedy of how God
verily comes to seek His own, and His own know Him
not. In the Fifth Century B. C., Empedocles, the
Greek philosopher who held the atomic theory, took
to himself the credit of being the first to understand
the nature of love and to recognize its true place in
human affairs. He was trying to find out the elements
of which the world was composed, and by what

processes it was held together. In his list of elements he named fire, water, earth, air, and then went on to say, "and love among them, their equal in length and breadth, her do thou fix in mental vision, nor sit with dazed eyes. She it is who is also thought to be implanted in the mortal members, making them think kindly thoughts and do friendly deeds. They call her Joy and Aphrodite. Her has no mortal yet observed among the elements of the world." A century afterward, in the most brilliant period of philosophy in Greece, Plato's soul was kindled to generous indignation by Empedocles's words, and with a burst of eloquence he protested against the heartlessness of the wisdom of his age: "What a strange thing it is that whereas other gods have poems and hymns made in their honour, the great and glorious god Love has no encomiast! The wise have descanted in prose on the virtues of Hercules and other heroes and have even made the utility of salt the theme of eloquent discourse, and only to think that there should have been an eager interest created about such things, and yet to this day no one has ever yet dared worthily to hymn Love's praises, so entirely has this great Deity been neglected." I think it was in his discourse on courage, "Lachesis," that he said that to injure anyone, even the most despised slave, was an affront to the holy bond which united gods and men and things in friendship. Then, except for the Voice of Divine Love speaking its message to the hate-dulled ears of men, more than twenty centuries passed with only here and there a mind brave enough to heed those heavenly accents and attempt to translate them into the harsh speech of earth. St. Augustine, Thomas Aquinas, à Kempis (whose "Meditations" I have read with joy), Spinoza, Jacob Boehme, and some other mystics and Francis Bacon stood valiantly on the outskirts of their time and gazed deeply into the vast, unknown sea of feeling which rolls forever beneath the darkness of words not understood. They had penetrating insight into the ways and works of love, love of others and self-love. It was Boehme who called the gnawing, burning appetites and desires of the selfish "the dark worm of hell"; of which the Scripture says, "their worm dieth not, and their fire is not quenched."

But only when Swedenborg arose out of the cold age of reason called the Eighteenth Century, did love as a doctrine again shine forth as the centre and life, the beauty and the preserver of all things. With the Bible for his authority, he developed this doctrine to some extent in his "Arcana Cœlestia" and more completely and systematically in his "Divine Love and Wisdom." He interpreted the whole world of human experience in terms of love—states of love —the activities, powers, and functions of love, the constructive, preventive, and courage-stirring dictates of love. Moreover, the seer discovered that love in the eminent sense is identical with the Divine itself, "that the Lord flows into the spirits of angels and men," that the material universe is God's Love wrought into forms suitable to the uses of life, and that the Word of God, rightly understood, reveals the fulness and the wonder of His Love toward all the children of men. Thus at last a faint ray, travelling through infinity from the Divine Soul, reached the mind of deaf, blind humanity, and lo, the second coming of the Lord was at hand.

Swedenborg's teachings about life can best be understood if we carefully differentiate between life and existence. The Lord bestows existence upon each of us for the express purpose of imparting life to us. His infinite Love impels Him to be a Creator, since love must have objects to which it can give its wealth of good-will and beneficence. In the Love which is the life of the Lord, we find the origin of creation. His infinite want cannot be satisfied with anything less than the existence of beings who can be finite recipients of His own happiness. At the same time such beings must have freedom and that rationality which accompanies true freedom. That is, His gift of life to men must be received voluntarily and thoughtfully by them if it is to be their own. That is why human beings pass through two distinct experiences—the birth into existence and the birth into life.

When we are born of the flesh, we are utterly

helpless and dependent, while in the spiritual birth we are active, and in a sense creators. We have nothing to do with our birth into existence; for we must exist before we can make anything of ourselves. On the other hand, our birth into life is a matter of choice, we have a very direct share in it; for no real spiritual life can be thrust upon us against our will.

This is the meaning of the Lord's constant, loving invitation through His Word to all of us, to come unto Him and choose life, and be ever on our guard against the evils which would rob us of the chosen life. Only by exercising our powers of thought and keeping our hearts always warm and pure do we become truly alive. But this beautiful work of re-creation cometh not by observation, it is wrought in the quiet depths of the soul. For, as the Lord says, "The wind bloweth where it listeth, and thou hearest the sound thereof, but thou canst not tell whence it cometh and whither it goeth; so is everyone that is born of the spirit."

Therefore we should not think of conversion as the acceptance of a particular creed, but as a change of heart. It is the soul turning away from the ignoble instincts which tempt us to feel, think, speak, and act for mere self-interest and the good opinion of the world, and finding joy in the unselfish love of God and a life of usefulness to others above all things. Our choice of life is this delight—this sweet expan-

sion of mind and heart withoout which no worth-
while achievement is possible.

But we are not born again all of a sudden, as
some people seem to think. It is a change which
comes over us as we hope and aspire and persevere
in the way of the Divine Commandments. For a
long time we resolve like angels, but drop back into
the old, matter-of-fact way of life, and do just what
we did before, like mortals. We are already on the
road to success, however, when we see that because
we have always done something, and because every-
body does it, and because our grandfathers did it,
are not good reasons why we should do it. There is
no plane of experience where, if we want to, we
cannot enlarge our lives by caring about people
outside ourselves, and seeking highest, most helpful
ideas of Him who is the "Way, the Truth, and the
Life." When once we make up our minds to do this,
and set out fearlessly, all outward circumstances and
limitations give way before us. We take up our cross
daily with a stronger heart and a fairer prospect of
life and happiness.

Swedenborg's own mind expanded slowly to the
higher light, and with deep suffering. The theological
systems of his day were little more than controver-
sies, and so full of long-drawn-out hair-splittings that
they seemed like caverns in which one would easily
get lost and never find one's way out again. Swedenborg had to define important keywords such as

*truth, soul, will, state, faith,* and give new meanings
to many other words so that he might translate more
of spiritual thought into common language. For his
doctrine of love he had to find a special vocabulary;
indeed, it almost seemed as if he were himself learning a different language. He was baffled by habits
of thought which any man accustomed to depend
largely on his eyes would require great courage
to break, so firmly are they entrenched in the sense.
It was one thing for him to perceive as through a
glass, darkly, the spiritual forces that sustain life,
and quite another thing for him to trace them clearly
back to their beautiful origin in the Heart of Love
and communicate them to an age of cold reason,
disputing creeds and skeptical inquiry. Trying to
"think the thoughts of God after Him," as Keplar
said, was a superhuman task. The only way I know
to give any idea of what Swedenborg was up against
is to suggest the tremendous obstacles a blind man
encounters when he wishes to help others handicapped like himself. He must spend his life trying
more or less successfully to make the seeing understand the particular needs of the sightless, and
the right method to repair their broken lives with
friendship, work, and happiness. It is amazing what
profound ignorance prevails even among fairly well-
informed persons regarding the blind, their feelings
and desires and capabilities. The seeing are apt to
conclude that the world of the blind—and especially

the deaf blind person—is quite unlike the sunlit, blooming world they know, that his feelings and sensations are essentially different from their own, and that his mental consciousness is fundamentally affected by his infirmities. They blunder still further, and imagine that he is shut out from all beauty of colour, music, and shape. They need to be told over and over innumerable times that the elements of beauty, order, form, and proportion, are tangible for the blind, and that beauty and rhythm are the result of a spiritual law deeper than sense. Yet how many people with eyes do take this truth to heart? How many of them take the trouble to ascertain for themselves the fact that the deaf-blind inherit their brain from a seeing and hearing race fitted for five senses, and the spirit fills the silent darkness with its own sunshine and harmony?

Now Swedenborg had a multitude of similar diffi-culties in conveying his impressions as a seer to the matter-clogged, mirage-filled senses of his genera-tion. Who knows—perhaps the limitations of the blind who have eyes and the deaf who have ears may yet be a means of carrying God's messages down into the darkest places of man's ignorance and insensibility. Without wishing to be the least bit pre-sumptuous, I hope I may have some skill to use helpfully my experience of life in the dark, as Swe-denborg used the experiences of two worlds which he said were granted him to elucidate the hidden meanings of the Old and the New Testaments. It is a peculiar happiness to me to bear record of the potency of God's Love and its creature, man's love, which stand between me and utter isolation, and make my misfortunes a medium of help and good-will to others. It is an ever-new sorrow to me to realize the tragedy of Swedenborg's opening words in the "Divine Love and Wisdom": "Man knows that there is such a thing as love; but he does not know what love is. . . . And because one is unable, when he reflects upon it, to form to himself any idea of thought about it, he says either that it is not any-thing, or that it is merely something flowing in from sight, hearing, touch, or intercourse with others, and thus affecting him. He is wholly unaware that love is very life; not only the common life of his whole body, and the common life of all his thoughts, but also the life of all their particulars. This a man of discernment can perceive when it is said; if you re-move the affection which is from love, can you think anything or do anything? Do not thought, speech, and action grow cold in the measure in which the affection which is from love grows cold? And do they not grow warm in the measure in which this affection grows warm? But this a man of discernment perceives only by observing that such is the case, and not from any knowledge that love is the life of man."

The trouble is, people mistake the utterances,

smiles, glances, and gentle deeds of love for love itself. It is just as if I should make the mistake of supposing that the brain thinks from its own power, or the body acts of its own accord, or the voice and tongue cause their own vibrations, or my hand recognizes anything independently of me, when really all these parts of the body are acted upon by the will and mind. Or as if I might place my hand on a beautiful lily and inhale its fragrance, and insist that the senses of touch and smell were in the flower, when in reality the skin by which I feel produces these sensations. That is the kind of appearances that should be guarded against when love, life, and mental activities are discussed. The common idea of love is that it is something outside of man—an entity floating about—a vague sentiment—one of the abstractions that cannot be talked about, because it cannot be distinctly thought about. But Swedenborg teaches that love is not an abstraction without cause, subject, or form. It does not float through the soul or come into being at the touch or sight of an object. It is the inmost essence of man out of which his spiritual organism is formed, and what we perceive as love is only a sign of that substance. Love actually keeps his faculties alive, as the atmosphere gives the senses of touch, smell, taste, sight, and hearing their sentient life.

I may illustrate the distinction between love and its tokens, for which it is so often mistaken. For, unless we have a vivid sense of love's reality, we cannot reach it and change or deepen or purify it, so that our affections may be higher, and our joy increased. We simply go round and round it in a vicious circle trying to change our tendencies, reconstruct ourselves and others, while love weeps at being left out—or if it be evil, it scoffs at us and hugs itself complacently. From my own struggle with imperfect speech I have this example of a wrong, roundabout, indirect method of making over what is marred. It would be absurd to attempt to improve my voice by operating on the sounds it emits as they float through the air. No, I must practise on my vocal organs, and that is of no use either until I improve my inner, or mental, concepts of speech. Voice is not essentially physical, it is thought making itself audible. It is literally shaped, tinted, and modulated by the mind. My supreme effort in practising is to get true images of sounds and words as it were in my internal ear, since my bodily ear is closed, and the nearer I approach the right use of mind as a speech instrument the better I shall be understood by others. This seems a far cry from voice to love; but the principle is exactly the same. Life, with all its emotions, likes, dislikes, and interests, flows, is moulded, coloured, and ultimately its vicissitudes are controlled, by the inmost love of man. He should strive to form the true mental concept of love as an active, creating, and dictating power if he wishes to acquire nobler feelings, finer ideals, and satisfy his so pathetic yearning for happiness.

Love should not be viewed as a detached effect of the soul or an organ or a faculty or a function. It involves the whole body of conscious thought, intention, purpose, endeavour, motives, and impulses, often suppressed, but always latent, ready at any moment to embody itself in act. It takes on face, hands, and feet through the faculties and organs; it works and talks, and will not be checked by any external circumstance, when once it would move toward an objective.

A very real regeneration comes with the change which begins in a man when he becomes conscious of his spiritual faculties. Such a change takes place not only after periods of bereavement and sorrow, but often after experiences of which he alone may be aware. There comes a day when his eyes are cleared, and he sees himself, his present environment, and the future in their true relations. The scales of selfishness fall away, and he looks at his own life soberly.

It is amazing how prodigiously men have written and talked about regeneration, and yet how little they have said to the purpose. Self-culture has been loudly and boastfully proclaimed as sufficient for all our ideals of perfection. But if we listen to the best men and women everywhere, they will answer with a decided negative. Some of them have amassed vast treasures of knowledge, and they will say that science may have found a cure for most evils; but it has found no remedy for the worst of them all—the apathy of human beings. It is pointed out, and Swedenborg says the same thing, that man, unschooled in love and pity, is worse than a beast. He is a hornless, tailless animal; he does not eat grass; but he wantonly destroys with his reckless power of thought. He invents more and more horrible weapons to kill and mar his brother man in war; he mutilates helpess animals for the changing sport of fashion; and he has a passion for fault-finding and scandal which rises beyond his control. Many other evils are no doubt traceable to his ignorance, but certainly not these pernicious tendencies. His deliverance is not going to be through self-culture unaided by right desires.

There is another large group of well-meaning people who hold that man can be reformed largely by a change of environment; and there is enough truth in this to render it plausible and attractive. But it is over-emphasized and often wrongly applied. It is not environment that alters a human being, but forces within him. The blind, the deaf, the prisoner for conscience' sake, even the poorest men with sound ideals, have all proved that they can shape life nearer to their desires, no matter what the outward circumstance.

Because there is a good deal of the child in us, we grow impatient easily and say to ourselves, "Oh, if we could stand in the lot of our more fortunate neighbours, we could live better, happier, and more useful lives." How often we hear a young man say, "If I had the opportunity of my boss's son, I could achieve great success." "If I didn't have to associate with such vulgar folk, I could become morally strong," says another, and a third laments, "If I only had the money of my wealthy friend, I should gladly do my part in the uplift of the world."

Now I am as much up in arms against needless poverty and degrading influences as anyone else, but, at the same time, I believe human experience teaches that if we cannot succeed in our present position, we could not succeed in any other. Unless, like the lily, we can rise pure and strong above sordid surroundings, we would probably be moral weaklings in any situation. Unless we can help the world where we are, we could not help it if we were somewhere else. The most important question is not the sort of environment we have, but the kind of thoughts we think every day, the kind of ideals we are following, in a word, the kind of men and women we really are. The Arab proverb is admirably true: "That is thy world wherein thou findest thyself."

Swedenborg has all these different theories in mind when he makes it clear that human beings cannot be regenerated suddenly without doing terrible violence to their minds and their self-esteem. They must advance step by step, accustoming their inner eyes to a keener light before they can endure the dazzle of new truths, and they cannot be turned toward a good life except by their delights. For it is these delights that keep them free and at last give them power to choose. Coöperation with the Lord and confidence in His unwearying help, learning to understand more truths in the Word and living according to them and doing good for its own sake—these are the only wholesome ways for mortals to rise out of their old selves and rebuild their world. They are greatly to be pitied if they wish to steal the merits of Christ or demand heaven as a "reward." It is much nobler for them to look into their own hearts and drive out the dragon of selfishness; this repentance they can accomplish quickly, but they must grow slowly and as cheerfully as possible, or they will never acquire any abiding strength of character. In fact, they will never stop regenerating in this life or the next, since they will forever find more to love, more to know, more to achieve.

# VII

SWEDENBORG'S sayings about delight and happiness seem as numberless as the flowers and leaves of a fruit tree in full bloom; and that is not surprising when he declares that the life of man is in the delight of what he loves. There is no interest where the heart is cold, and where there is no impulse, there is no delight. Human happiness is composed of countless small joys, just as time is made up of minutes and seconds; but few people with all their senses stop to think of this, and still fewer sit down to count their blessings. If they did, they would be kept so busy that the next harsh call to duty would seem music to their enchanted ears.

I do not refer to hedonism, which is seeking happiness as an end, and not usefulness. So I hope my words will not seem light to any earnest person when I speak of the universe as a table spread by Divine beneficence with a feast to the soul. Every faculty of the mind and every appetite of the body have their delights, which are the means of renewal and upbuilding. Every single power in man's nature, physical and mental, should have a chance to choose and appropriate to itself what is congenial and satisfying. It is not necessary, as is very often supposed, to give up natural pleasures before we can gain spiritual ones. On the contrary, we enjoy them more exquisitely as we rise in the inner life. How wonderful is a bunch of grapes sent by a dear friend —its rounded beauty and colour and its delicious fragrance, with love, imagination, and poetry over and above! How rich and varied we find flowers in fragrant delights that quicken the brain and open our heart-blossoms! How endlessly the changes of sky and water and earth charm us and keep before us a lovely mirror of the higher world upon which our faith and our dreams are centered!

This world is so full of care and sorrow that it is a gracious debt we owe to one another to discover the bright crystals of delight hidden in sombre circumstances and irksome tasks. Swedenborg, whose labours were a giant's, saw inexhaustible stores of joy in the midst of exacting routine. Out of his heart and out of heaven's heart he wrote in the "True Christian Religion":

"The joys of love, which are also the joys of charity, cause what is good to be called good; and the charms of wisdom, which are also the charms of faith, cause what is true to be called true; for joys and charms of various kinds make their life, and without life from these, goods and truths are like inanimate things, and are also unfruitful."

"The love whose joy is essentially good is like the heat of the sun, fructifying, vivifying, and operating on a fertile soil, on fruit trees and fields of

corn, and where it operates there is produced, as
it were, a paradise, a garden of Jehovah, and a land
of Canaan; and the charm of its truth is as the light
of the sun in the time of spring, and as light flowing
into a crystal vessel in which are beautiful flowers,
from which as they open breathes forth a fragrant
perfume."

As selfishness and complaint pervert and cloud the
mind, so love with its joy clears and sharpens the
vision. It gives the delicacy of perception to see
wonders in what before seemed dull and trivial. It
replenishes the springs of inspiration, and its joy
sends a new river of life like blood through the
matter-clogged faculties.

There is a growing sentiment among thoughtful
people that delight is essential to growth and self-
improvement and the acquisition of nobler instincts.
What induces a child to learn but his delight in
knowing? Do not the pleasures of taste enable the
body to assimilate food? What mind that thinks at
all does not choose the ideas which please it and let
all others go unheeded? What does a man do with
his secret inner will but fix it upon some El Dorado
which allures him, and wait until he can realize his
dream? What is it but dreaming the delight that
leads the brave and the adventurous on to fresh
discoveries and the increase of man's natural
resources? Why does the scientist often endure
mental travail and repulsive tasks, if not for the

delight he feels in understanding new truths or rendering a new service to others? A wise teacher or friend or true reformer does not attempt to drag a wrong-doer into the right way by force. He skilfully combines discipline with pleasant influences that may soften the stubborn will and charm the sullen mind into right thinking. Anyone who, out of goodness of his heart, speaks a helpful word, gives a cheering smile, or smooths over a rough place in another's path, knows that the delight he feels is so intimate a part of himself that he lives by it. The joy of surmounting obstacles which once seemed unremovable, and pushing the frontier of accomplishment further—what joy is there like unto it? If those who seek happiness would only stop one little minute and think, they would see that the delights they really experience are as countless as the grasses at their feet or the dewdrops sparkling upon the morning flowers.

Yet how few persons I meet realize this wealth of joy! It is a marvel and a sorrow to me to observe how far afield they go in pursuit of happiness. They look for it in the strangest of places. They visit kings and queens and bow to them; they seek happiness in travel and excitement; they dig for it into the depths of the earth, thinking that it lies in hidden treasure. Many others rob themselves of joy by superstitiously fettering their intellect for the sake of religion or convention or party policy. Most pitiably are they blinded, deafened, and starved when all the time there is within them a world of sweet wealth ready to bless their hearts and minds. It is God's good gift to them out of His Happiness, and they know it not.

To help a man to find himself is often to surprise him with new-found joy. For delight serves as a means of self-knowledge. Swedenborg says, if a man will examine his own delights, he will often realize that he is self-centered because most of his energies are directed to shaping his own life or acquiring knowledge for his private ends; but it turns out that his more enduring joys are born of an unselfish purpose to serve others and create new life in the world. These selfless delights will whisper approval to him, and he will rise thrice a man because he is conscious of new powers and new self insights. Only when you trace the footsteps of your spirit to the home of its delights shall you behold your own form and face and read your fate in the Book of Life.

But Swedenborg also says that if a man with unlovely delights has the intellectual honesty to acknowledge them, and earnestly tries to lift up his heart to something worthy, he need not, he must not, despair. As fast as his old fascinations depart, pure happiness will rush into his soul as irresistibly as strong air currents which gladden a long shut-up dwelling, and the happier he becomes, the stronger he will be to remould outward circumstances to his desire. It is a mistake for him to entertain fears about the enemy finding a breach in his once broken ramparts. In place of each fear he can build a new delight and stay his mind upon it until the ordeal passes. That is what is meant by "a hobby" in modern thought, and it is wonderful to read how many unfortunate men and women are being thus helped out of seemingly hopeless evil tendencies into undreamed self-development, a heaven-given psycho-therapy. Forgiveness for sin is nothing but the well-spring of joy from above that fills the bruised heart when one has driven out wrong desires and evil thoughts, and works in harmony with the powers of good.

It is beyond a doubt that everyone should have time for some special delight, if only five minutes each day to seek out a lovely flower or cloud or a star, or learn a verse or brighten another's dull task. What is the use of such terrible diligence as many tire themselves out with, if they always postpone their exchange of smiles with Beauty and Joy to cling to irksome duties and relations? Unless they admit these fair, fresh, and eternal presences into their lives as they can, they must needs shut themselves out of heaven, and a gray dust settles on all existence. That the sky is brighter than the earth means little unless the earth itself is appreciated and enjoyed. Its beauty loved gives the right to aspire to the radiance of the sunrise and the stars.

Few people are saints or geniuses; but there is always this much of hope in all men—every pure delight they cherish is as "focus of good-will," and every lovely scene they dwell on, every harmony they listen to, every graceful or tender thing they touch with reverent hand starts on the wing a flock of sweet thoughts which neither care nor poverty nor pain can destroy. Joy is the voice of the love and faith that shall at last pronounce the word of eternal life—"Well done!"

Joy is inseparable from the doctrines set forth by Swedenborg. In that day his was a new branch of philosophy that seemed strange after the penances of the Middle Ages and the gloom of iron creeds. One of the surprises of his teaching is the universality of delight as a minister to life. His superb faith in man's ability to augment the happiness of marriage and to make the life of childhood beautiful is still far ahead of the timid distrust, the low ideals, and the stupid methods of imparting knowledge which prevail among us. In a word, true life is the heart's capacity for joy fulfilled.

We are beginning to perceive the Divine Providence as Swedenborg describes it—in a circle of large, noble ideas which are consistent with its greatness. Heretofore it has been darkened by controversial dogmas, and often its meaning has degenerated into special provisions which imply special neglects. But in Swedenborg's teaching it is shown to be the government of God's Love and Wisdom and the creation of uses. Since His Life cannot be less in one being than another, or His Love manifested less fully in one thing than another, His Providence must needs be universal.

One of the neglects which used to be pointed out was the exclusion of vast multitudes from the blessings of salvation through Jesus Christ. This idea, however, is giving way to a more generous understanding that God has "other sheep who hear His Voice and obey Him." He has provided religion of some kind everywhere, and it does not matter to what race or creed anyone belongs if he is faithful to his ideals of right living. The one principle to be remembered by all is that religion is to live a doctrine, not merely to believe one. It was of the Divine Providence that Mohammed arose to overthrow idol-worship. This great prophet taught a form of religion adapted to the peculiar genius of Orientals, and that explains the mighty influence for good this faith has exercised in many empires and kingdoms. The history of religious thought proclaims in trumpet tones that God has never left Himself without a witness.

Wherever, as is the tendency of conventional worship, the dogmas of a nation turn wicked, simple good people abound who remain unharmed by them because they are far from the corruption in high places.

If we view the Divine Providence from the heaven in our minds, past experiences yield up to us precious lessons of wisdom and helpfulness, and we feel the harmony of life; but if we look at God's ways from a world of accident, chance, and discord, we misunderstand them utterly. We regard Him as an arbitrary dispenser of rewards and punishments, partial to favourites and vengeful to adversaries. We presume upon His immensity with our petty patriotisms and pray to Him for victory. We turn to warring sects—and where is He? It has even been said to me, "If there were a God, would He not have created man so that he could never sin?" As if anybody wished him to be an automaton. Not to be able to sin could satisfy only a despot; does not the spirit shiver at such a concept? In fact, all denials of God are found at last to be denials of freedom and humanity. The living value of a belief depends not on our own limited experience but on its benefit to mankind; and an overruling Beneficence is the only teaching that ultimately justifies our knowledge or gives dignity to civilization. It includes many gifts, but above all the power of going out of oneself and appreciating whatever is noble in man and wonderful in the universe.

Swedenborg's "Divine Providence" is a powerfully personal testimony to the truth that God created the universe because of the infinite need of His nature to give life and joy. The futility and hollowness of belief in a remote, unapproachable Deity is shown in many a passage of that comforting work. The author declares that "It is the essence of God's Love to love others, to desire to be one with them, and from Himself to make them happy." That is the whole of the Divine Providence, and we must let ourselves be borne along by it as by a current if we wish to accomplish our part in His Work of spiritual rehabilitation.

Therefore in the vicissitudes of our lives the Divine Providence looks, not to temporal blessings only, but chiefly to our eternal welfare and happiness. The million little things that drop into our hands, the small opportunities each day brings He leaves us free to use or abuse and goes unchanging along His silent way; yet always He guards the right of everyone to act in freedom according to reason. For liberty and rationality are tokens of His gift of immortality to human kind.

Since we are all too prone to live selfishly, it is necessary that there should be something within us to offset this tendency. The choice of a better life which we are to make involves some previous knowledge of such a life. What could save us from

becoming more and more like animals, if there were
not present with us other tendencies of a nobler
kind? We cannot freely and wisely choose the right
way for ourselves unless we know both good and
evil.

This is all said to explain Swedenborg's doctrine
of "reliquiæ" as a powerful factor in moulding life.
That word, often translated "remains," signifies the
lasting impressions of love and truth and beauty left
in us from the days of our childhood. At birth we
are passive. Our inherited evil tendencies are as yet
quiescent. That is why the little child is so near to
heaven, and we so often feel that the angels are
ministering to him. "Their angels do always behold
the face of my Father which is in heaven." Truly,
the child comes in "trailing clouds of glory," with
characteristics and potentialities different from any
other human being. He receives capabilities of goodness and wisdom from the Lord alone, and in a
very real sense heaven enspheres him like the sunshine. This is the way Swedenborg accounts for the
beautiful innocence and trust of the little child. We
never completely lose this innocence and trust. Our
stored-up capabilities are the holy places where we
feel our kinship with the Divine. These are the
places of sacrifice, the meeting-ground of mortal
and immortal, the tents of trial where are waged
the great spiritual combats of man's life. Here are

the tears and agonies and the bloody sweat of Geth-
semane. Happy the man who can say to himself,
"Here, too, was the victory!" Here is the shrine of
the life we have chosen.

# VIII

O NCE affliction was looked upon as a punishment from God—a burden to be borne passively and piously. The only idea of helping the victims of misfortune was to shelter them and leave them to meditate and live as contentedly as possible in the valley of the shadow. But now we understand that a sequestered life without aspiration enfeebles the spirit. It is exactly the same as with the body. The muscles must be used, or they lose their strength. If we do not go out of our limited experience somehow and use our memory, understanding, and sympathy, they become inactive. It is by fighting the limitations, temptations, and failures of the world that we reach our highest possibilities. That is what Swedenborg calls renouncing the world and worshipping God.

Sick or well, blind or seeing, bond or free, we are here for a purpose and however we are situated, we please God better with useful deeds than with many prayers or pious resignation. The temple or church is empty unless the good of life fills it. It is not the stone walls that make it small or large, but the brave soul's light shining round about. The altar is holy if only it represents the altar of our heart upon which we offer the only sacrifices ever commanded—the love that is stronger than hate and the faith that overcometh doubt.

A simple, childlike faith in a Divine Friend solves all the problems that come to us by land or sea. Difficulties meet us at every turn. They are the accompaniment of life. They result from combinations of character and individual idosyncrasies. The surest way to meet them is to assume that we are immortal, and that we have a Friend who "slumbers not, nor sleeps," and who watches over us and guides us—if we but let Him. With this thought strongly intrenched in our inmost being, we can do almost anything we wish and need not limit the things we think. We may help ourselves to all the beauty of the universe that we can hold. For every hurt there is recompense of tender sympathy. Out of pain grow the violets of patience and sweetness, the vision of the Holy Fire that touched the lips of Isaiah and kindled his life into spirit, and the contentment that comes with the evening star. The marvellous richness of human experience would lose something of rewarding joy if there were no limitations to overcome. The hilltop hour would not be half so wonderful if there were no dark valley to traverse.

I have never believed that my limitations were in any sense punishments or accidents. If I had held such a view, I could never have exerted the strength to overcome them. It has always seemed to me that there is a very special significance in the words of "the Epistle of Paul to the Hebrews": "If we are chastened, God dealeth with us as with sons." Swedenborg's teachings bear me out in this view. He defines the greatly misunderstood word chastening or chastisement, not as punishment, but as training, discipline, refinement of the soul.

The "True Christian Religion" is full of stimuli for faith in our God-given powers and self-activity. The chapters "Faith" and "Free-will" are a powerful declaration that we should never surrender to misfortunes or circumstances or even to our faults hopelessly, passively—as if we were but carved images with our hands hanging down, waiting for God's Grace to put us into motion. We should give no quarter to spiritual slavery. We should take the initiative, look into ourselves fearlessly, search out new ideas of what to do, and ways to develop our willpower. Then God will give us enough light and love for all our needs.

Now, limitations of all kinds are forms of chastening to encourage self-development and true freedom. They are tools put into our hands to hew away the stone and flint which keep the higher gifts hidden away in our being. They tear away the bandage of indifference from our eyes, and we behold the burdens others are carrying, and we learn to help them by yielding to the dictates of a pitying heart.

The example of the newly blinded man is so concrete, I wish to use it as a type for all life-training.

When he first loses his sight, he thinks there is nothing left for him but heartache and despair. He feels shut out from all that is human. Life to him is like the ashes on a cold hearth. The fire of ambition is quenched. The light of hope is gone out. The objects in which he once took delight seem to thrust out sharp edges at him as he gropes his way about. Even those who love him act unwittingly as an irritant to his feelings because he can no longer give them the support of his labour. Then comes some wise teacher and friend and assures him he can work with his hands and to a considerable degree train his hearing to take the place of sight. Often the stricken man does not believe it, and in his despair interprets it as a mockery. Like a drowning person he strikes blindly at anyone that tries to save him. Nevertheless, the sufferer must be urged onward in spite of himself, and when he once realizes that he can put himself again in connection with the world, and fulfil tasks worthy of a man, a being he did not dream of before unfolds itself within him. If he is wise, he discovers at last that happiness has very little to do with outward circumstances, and he treads his dark way with a firmer will than he ever felt in the light.

Likewise those who have been mentally blinded "in the gradual furnace of the world" can, and must, be pressed to look for new capabilities within themselves and work out new ways to happiness.

They may even resent faith that expects nobler things from them. They say in effect, "I will be content if you take me for what I am—dull, or mean, or hard, or selfish." But it is an affront to them and to the eternal dignity of man so to acquiesce. How often it comes over us that there is much in us which our nearest friends cannot know—more than we dare or care or are able to lay bare, more of feeling, more of power, more of manhood. How little we know ourselves! We need limitations and temptations to open our inner selves, dispel our ignorance, tear off disguises, throw down old idols, and destroy false standards. Only by such rude awakenings can we be led to dwell in a place where we are less cramped, less hindered by the ever-insistent External. Only then do we discover a new capacity and appreciation of goodness and beauty and truth.

From such experience we may gain a wonderful interpretation of the Lord's words: "Verily, verily, I say unto you, he that receiveth whomsoever I send receiveth me." We may know that in every limitation we overcome and in the higher ideals we thus attain the whole kingdom of Love and Wisdom is present. In this way we learn that the real way to grow is by aspiring beyond our limitations, by wishing sublimely for great things and striving to achieve them. We grow in our increasing consciousness of the deeper meaning of the outer life in which we have always lived.

The eye grows by learning to see more in particular objects. To man's physical sight the earth looks flat, and the stars are the same to us that they were to the ancients. Yet science has opened up infinite new wonders and glories in these phenomena! A child sees in the things about him only what he wants or does not want, but when a Newton recognizes the falling of the apple as the expression of a universal force in Nature, he sees far beyond ordinary sight. It is the same with our spirits. We grow as we discern more fully the possibilities of new life wrapped up in daily contacts. But when we forget or ignore this vital fact, the senses lead us astray. That is why limitations are necessary to bring before us the greatness of inner life offered us in the circumstances of our lives, and show us our God-given opportunities.

The constant service of Swedenborg lies in such thoughts as these. He shows us that in every event and every limitation we have a choice, and that to choose it is to create. We can decide to let our trials crush us, or we can convert them to new forces of good. We can drift along with general opinion and tradition, or we can throw ourselves upon the guidance of the soul within and steer courageously toward truth. We cannot tell from the outside whether our experiences are really blessings or not. They are cups of poison, or cups of healthful life, according to what we ourselves put into them. The choices offered us are never so much between what we may or may not do, as between the principles from which we act when we are thwarted and limited. Earth is not intended to be an altogether delighful abode any more than it is to be a place of wrath. Since the soil brings forth thistles, and roses have thorns, why should man's life not have its trials? It is not strange, or cruel. It is the urge of God that impels us to enlarge our lives and keep strong for that higher destiny which cannot be accomplished within the limits of earth. Only by striving for what is beyond us do we win expansion and joy. Let us, then, take up that limitation which each one has, and follow the example of Him who bore upon his frail human shoulders the cross of the world, that He might become a luminous and inspiring influence, communicating life-giving thoughts and desires to the weak, the tempted, and the despondent.

I do not know if it is the "mystic" sense I possess; but certainly it is perceptive. It is the faculty that brings distant objects within the cognizance of the blind so that even the stars seem to be at our very door. This sense relates me to the spiritual world. It surveys the limited experience I gain from an imperfect touch world, and presents it to my mind for spiritualization. This sense reveals the Divine to the human in me, it forms a bond between earth and the Great Beyond, between now and eternity, between God and man. It is speculative, intuitive, reminiscent

There is not only an objective physical world, but also an objective spiritual world. The spiritual has an outside as well as an inside, just as the physical has an inside and an outside. Each has its own phase of reality. There is no antagonism between these two planes of life, except when the material is used without regard to the spiritual which lies within and above it. The distinction between them is explained by Swedenborg in his theory of discrete degrees. He illustrates this by saying that the physical world is perceived by a sensory apparatus that is of the same substance as the physical world, while the spiritual world is perceived by a sensory apparatus that is of the same substance as that of the spiritual world.

My life is so complicated by a triple handicap of blindness, deafness, and imperfect speech that I cannot do the simplest thing without thought and effort to rationalize my experiences. If I employed this mystic sense constantly without trying to understand the outside world, my progress would be checked, and everything would fall about me in chaos. It is easy for me to mix up dreams and reality, the spiritual and the physical which I have not properly visualized, and without the inner sense I could not keep them apart. So even if I commit errors in forming concepts of colour, sound, light, and intangible phenomena, I must always try to preserve equilibrium between my outer and inner life. Neither can I use my sense of touch without regard to the experience of others and respect for it. I should otherwise go astray or else go round and round in a blind circle. I have always been especially helped by this sentence from Swedenborg's "Arcana Cœlestia":

"It is the interior man that sees and perceives what goes on without him, and from this interior source the sense-experience has its life; for from no other than this subjective source is there any faculty of feeling or sensation. But the fallacy that the sense comes from without is of such a nature and so common that the natural mind cannot rid itself of it, nor even the rational mind, until it can think abstractly from sense."

When the sun of consciousness first shone upon me, behold a miracle! The stock of my young life which had perished, steeped in the waters of knowledge grew again, budded again, was sweet again with the blossoms of childhood! Down in the depths of my being I cried, "It is good to be alive!" I held out two trembling hands to life, and in vain silence would impose dumbness upon me henceforth! The world to which I awoke was still mysterious; but there were hope and love and God in it, and nothing else mattered. Is it not possible that our entrance into heaven may be like this experience of mine?

Several years later my life enlarged when I learned to speak. I can never cease to marvel and be excited by that event of thirty-six years ago, it stands out so isolated, miraculous, baffling. Think of transforming mute, soulless air into speech in the midst of midnight silence. Literally, I had no concepts of speech, and my touch did not suffice to convey to me the thousand fine vibrations of spoken words. Without physical hearing I had to exert the utmost thought of which I was capable until I succeeded in making myself not only heard but understood! It is only by sheer force of mind even now that I keep my speech anywhere near intelligible. When I speak best, I am at a loss to fix that degree of perfection because I cannot fully sense the tones going forth from my lips. What surprises me is not that I fail, but that the subconscious part or the spirit enters so often into my clumsy speech, and my friends say earnestly, "Why can you not talk as well as that always?" If I could develop that psychic power more fully, I feel sure that my victory would be complete. The pain and disappointment I have endured are incalculable; but they are a price worth paying for the joy I have in being able to keep this living bond between the outer world and myself. As I learned to articulate and to put feeling into what I said I sensed more and more the miracle of all time and eternity—the reality of thought! Thought, out of which are wrought books, philosophies, sciences, civilizations, and the joy and the woe of the human race! Even as if the lonely blind man who has travelled many years in midnight gloom should suddenly stumble upon the

sun and all the glories of a sunlit world, so it was
with me when the light of understanding flooded my
mind, and I realized that words were precious symbols of knowledge, thought, and happiness. The
normal human being is familiar with the use of
words, and he cannot remember when he first began
to use them. I have had a different experience. I was
nearly seven years old when I began to acquire language, and I remember distinctly the feelings I ex-
perienced. I learned each word as a hand-sensation
years before I learned the sound of it. With most
people the sound and the perception of the meanings
of the word are, I suppose, simultaneous. The
significance of thought-symbols came to me suddenly.

My teacher, Anne Mansfield Sullivan, had been
with me nearly a month, and she had taught me the
names of a number of objects. She put them into
my hand, spelled their names on her fingers and
helped me to form the letters; but I had not the
faintest idea what I was doing. I do not know what I
thought. I have only a tactual memory of my fingers
going through those motions, and changing from one
position to another. One day she handed me a cup
and spelled the word. Then she poured some liquid
into the cup and formed the letters w-a-t-e-r. She says
I looked puzzled, and persisted in confusing the two
words, spelling cup for water and water for cup.
Finally I became angry because Miss Sullivan kept

repeating the words over and over again. In despair she led me out to the ivy-covered pump-house and made me hold the cup under the spout while she pumped. With her other hand she spelled w-a-t-e-r emphatically. I stood still, my whole body's attention fixed on the motions of her fingers as the cool stream flowed over my hand. All at once there was a strange stir within me—a misty consciousness, a sense of something remembered. It was as if I had come back to life after being dead! I understood that what my teacher was doing with her fingers meant that the cold something that was rushing over my hand was water, and that it was possible for me to communicate with other people by these hand signs. It was a wonderful day never to be forgotten! Thoughts that ran forward and backward came to me quickly —thoughts that seemed to start in my brain and spread all over me. Now I see it was my mental awakening. I think it was an experience somewhat in the nature of a revelation. I showed immediately in many ways that a great change had taken place in me. I wanted to learn the name of every object I touched, and before night I had mastered thirty words. Nothingness was blotted out! I felt joyous, strong, equal to my limitations! Delicious sensations rippled through me, and sweet, strange things that were locked up in my heart began to sing. That first revelation was worth all those years I had spent in dark, soundless imprisonment. That word "water" dropped into my mind like the sun in a frozen winter world. Before that supreme event there was nothing in me except the instinct to eat and drink and sleep. My days were a blank without past, present, or future, without hope or anticipation, without interest or joy.

It was not night—it was not day.
But vacancy **absorbing space,**
And fixedness, without a place:
There were no stars—no earth—no time—
No check—no change—no good—no crime.

It was but a step for me from the wonders of nature to the wonders of the spirit. When Swedenborg's message was revealed to me, it was another precious gift added to life. I will try to clothe my emotion in words. It was as if light came where there had been no light before, the intangible world became a shining certainty. The horizons of my mind widened to bright destinies where the race would still be swift, the battle strong.

Heaven, as Swedenborg portrays it, is not a mere collection of radiant ideas, but a practical, liveable world. It should never be forgotten that death is not the end of life, but only one of its most important experiences. In the great silence of my thoughts all those whom I have loved on earth, whether near or far, living or dead, live and have their own in**dividuality,** their own dear ways and charm. At any moment I can bring them around to me to cheer my loneliness. It would break my heart if any barrier could prevent them from coming to me. But I know there are two worlds—one we can measure with line and rule, and the other we can feel with our hearts and intuitions. Swedenborg makes the future life not only conceivable, but desirable. His message to the living who meet the might of death with its attendant separation and sorrow sweeps across the heart of humanity like some sweet breath from God's Presence. We can now meet death as Nature does, in a blaze of glory, marching to the grave with a gay step, wearing our brightest thoughts and most brilliant anticipations, as Nature arrays herself in garments of gold, emerald, and scarlet, as if defying death to rob her of immortality.

The difficulty man has in believing this arises not so much from the unprovableness of it as from his own incredulous attitude. His egoistic desires tend to overwhelm his spiritual strivings, or, perhaps, it is nearer the truth to say, his inner faculties have not yet reached the point of conscious experience. They are still too feeble to function effectively. He is unable to realize the pernicious influence of acquisitiveness upon his character. He does not understand the true significance of his spiritual being. He believes that only material things are real. Our civilization is a failure in the degree to which we are indifferent to the teachings of philosophers like Swedenborg and the visions of the great thinkers of the world.

With thoughts wide as the universe, deliberate, with wisdom in his hands, Swedenborg tells us how angels led him from realm to realm of the spirit-world, showed him the life that comes after death and the reality of things immortal. Angels wcre his teachers, his guides. He lodged his soul in heaven; he sensed the magnitude of the Divine Providence, the tremendous circumstance of life eternal. He was permitted to walk the sky and the winding course of stars.

I am aware that some learned critics will break me on the wheel of their disdain. They will try to mend my poor philosophy on the anvil of their keen mirth with the hammer of reasons culled from science. "All creation crowns itself in this invisible atom of matter. It is the beginning and the end." Perhaps; but there is still a dewdrop in the lily's cup; there is fragrance in the heart of the rose, and under a leaf a bird folds its wings! I cannnot understand the poor faith that fears to look into the eyes of death. Faith that is vulnerable in the presence of death is a frail reed to lean upon. With steadfast thought I follow sight beyond all seeing, until my soul stands up in spiritual light and cries, "Life and death are one." When I review my life, it seems to me that my most precious obligations are to those whom I have never seen. My dearest intimacies are those of the mind, my most loyal and helpful friends are those of the spirit.

I cannot imagine myself without religion. I could as easily fancy a living body without a heart. To one who is deaf and blind, the spiritual world offers no difficulty. Nearly everything in the natural world is as vague, as remote from my senses as spiritual things seem to the minds of most people. I plunge my hands deep into my large Braille volumes containing Swedenborg's teachings, and withdraw them full of the secrets of the spiritual world. The inner, or "mystic," sense, if you like, gives me vision of the unseen. My mystic world is lovely with trees and clouds and stars and eddying streams I have never "seen." I am often conscious of beautiful flowers and birds and laughing children where to my seeing associates there is nothing. They sceptically declare that I see "light that never was on sea or land." But I know that their mystic sense is dormant, and that is why there are so many barren places in their lives. They prefer "facts" to vision. They want a scientific demonstration and they can have it. Science with untiring patience traces man back to the ape, and rests content. It is out of this ape that God creates the seer, and science meets spirit as life meets death, and life and death are one.

## Swedenborg's Theological Works:

Apocalypse Explained, 6 volumes.

Apocalypse Revealed, 2 volumes.

Arcana Coelestia, 12 volumes.

Conjugial Love

Divine Love and Wisdom

Divine Providence

Four Doctrines

Heaven and Hell

Miscellaneous Theological Works

Posthumous Theological Works, 2 volumes.

The Spiritual Life, The Word of God

True Christian Religion, 2 volumes.

Spiritual Diary, 5 volumes.

## OTHER TITLES

**A Compendium of Swedenborg's Theological Writings** - Warren

**Blake & Swedenborg: Opposition is True Friendship** - Bellin and Ruhl

**The Essential Swedenborg** - Synnestvedt

**Introduction to Swedenborg's Religious Thought** - Spalding

**Language of Parable** - Worchester

**Natural Depth in Man** - Van Dusen

**Outlines of Swedenborg's Teachings** - Wunsch

**Presence of Other Worlds** - Van Dusen

**Swedenborg Epic** - Sigstedt

**View from Within: A Compendium** - Dole

Order from your bookdealer or send below for Free Catalogue:

Swedenborg Foundation, Inc.
Dept. MRC
139 East 23rd St.
New York, N.Y. 10010